Finding Out About Child Development

Finding Out About Child Development

Valda Reynolds Cert.Ed.

Joint Chief Examiner, Midland Examining Group
for GCSE Home Economics: Child Development

Stanley Thornes (Publishers) Ltd

Acknowledgements

The author and publishers would like to thank the following for their help in the production of this book: Gemma White, Birdlip County Primary School, Glos, for the cover picture; Peter Reynolds for typing the script, proof reading and compiling the index.

We would like to thank the following for permission to reproduce previously published material: Consumers' Association, Department of Trade and Industry, the Controller of Her Majesty's Stationery Office, Kidscape, Midlands Examining Group, NSPCC, Office of Population Censuses and Surveys (OPCS), *Practical Health* magazine, RoSPA; and photographs: Burton Daily Mail Ltd (p. 145); Sally and Richard Greenhill (pp. 58 bottom left, 86, 129); *The Irish Post* (p. 113); Mrs C Loose (p. 135 top right); Mothercare (p. 87); NSPCC (p. 143); Nursery World (p. 91, Bob Bray; p. 98, Bob Bray [top left, top middle, bottom middle], Pauline Cutler [top right], David Mansell [bottom right], Eric Riddick [bottom left]); RNIB Iain Jacobs (p. 135 bottom right); RNID (p. 135 top left); RoSPA (p. 79); Spastics Society/ Michelle Smith (p. 135 bottom left); Universal Press Syndicate © 1986 G B Trudeau (p. 101 cartoon); Vision International (p. 26); Janine Wiedel (pp. 44, 58 top left, top right, bottom right).

Every effort has been made to trace copyright holders and we apologise if any have been overlooked.

First published in 1989 by
Stanley Thornes (Publishers) Ltd
Old Station Drive
Leckhampton
CHELTENHAM GL53 0DN
England

Reprinted 1990

British Library Cataloguing in Publication Data

Reynolds, Valda
   Finding out about child development.
   1. Children. Development
   I. Title
   155.4

ISBN 0–85950–928–1

Typeset by Tech-Set, Gateshead, Tyne & Wear
Printed and bound in Great Britain at The Bath Press, Avon

Contents

How to Use this Book

Finding Out About Child Development has been designed to have an emphasis on active learning with a high degree of pupil involvement. The **Guidance** chapter at the beginning of the book explains the **skills** required for studying Child Development courses; methods of observing, investigating, recording and analysing information.

The rest of the book is divided into three **study areas** each of which is subdivided into a number of **units**. Each unit provides:

- a **core information** section
- a **pupil participation** section in the form of **working briefs** and **written work**. You will be able to add to the core information with research of your own to complete the work in this section. The work includes: discussions, surveys, investigations, fact-finding exercises, data response and free response questions.

As you complete each unit you should fill in a **self-assessment chart** and **self-marking plan** for that unit, so that you can assess your own progress. Copymasters of these forms are provided on pages 161 and 162 for you to photocopy.

Appendices appear at the end of each study area. These give examples of methods of recording and presenting results, and a resources guide. A list of useful addresses appears on page 159.

The **link-up charts** on pages 163–8 show how the subjects covered in this book are linked to the other common elements of GCSE Home Economics: Home, Food and Textiles. The charts also show at a glance which common themes and skills required for GCSE are provided in each study area.

Guidance

Skills

The **skills** which are needed when studying Child Development courses are:
- investigation
- measurement
- communication
- management
- psycho-motor
- technological
- interpersonal
- caring.

During your course you will be required to use and develop skills in these areas, and these will be tested in your coursework and theory papers. Pregnancy, birth, development of the child and family life are all continuing processes. You will need to:

Investigate
Why children act as they do at their various stages of development.
The products and facilities available to the pregnant woman, the child and the family.
The personnel involved in their care.

Observe
All the activities of babies and children.
Parents and families and how they tackle child rearing and family life.
People involved in child care and development, for example, medical personnel, playgroup leaders and teachers.
The places and facilities provided by the community, for example, information services, health and social services departments, and shopping areas and procedures.

Select and analyse your information
Set yourself some problem situations and use the information you have collected to provide possible solutions.
Your work can be of a practical nature, for example, a working brief with a completed item of practical work, or written work presented as a survey, child study or investigation.

Record your information
There are many ways of doing this, but make sure:
- it is clear
- it is neat
- it is well written or typed
- it is on suitable paper
- it is well mounted and includes appropriate photographs and cuttings
- there are large, clearly labelled drawings
- tapes are clearly audible
- it is easily understood
- you select only relevant information
- you use note form, charts and diagrams to cut down on extensive information
- it is interesting and original
- you do not copy long passages from books – interpret the information and put it in your own words
- you include an index and bibliography when appropriate
- you are accurate
- you use correct technical terms, which are correctly spelt.

Interpret and evaluate
Look at the work you have done:
Have you interpreted your initial instructions and requirements correctly?
Has your work achieved its purpose?
Has it offered solutions to a problem?
Did it involve you in active learning processes?

What skills have you used?
Have you learnt something new and of value?
Could you recall the information clearly and explain it to someone else?

Do a personal evaluation (ask yourself these questions)
Did this work interest me and stimulate me to further research?
Did other people achieve better results than I did, and if so, why?
Am I satisfied with my work?
How could my work have been improved?

Investigate → Observe → Select and analyse → Record → Interpret → Evaluate.

By following this process, you will be using and developing all the important skills.

Investigation

Investigate your subject by collecting together and using as many **resources** as you can.

Examples: collect leaflets, booklets, magazines, books, audio and visual tapes, worksheets, information sheets, catalogues, pictures, photographs and free samples; visit exhibitions and museums; invite outside speakers; listen to and watch relevant radio and TV programmes.

Sources: shops, manufacturers, voluntary organisations, Citizens Advice Bureaux (CABs), consumer centres, government departments, public libraries, post offices.

Important points are:

● Make letters of request short and polite, include a stamped, addressed envelope and send collectively if the whole group requires information.
● Always be on the look-out for information.
● Request permission before you go to look round shops or visit baby clinics, playgroups, etc.
● Use your time sensibly when on visits and make notes of what you see and hear.
● Always be polite, even if others are less than polite to you.

Observation

There is a difference between 'looking' and 'observing'. If you just look at something you will receive an impression which is quickly gone. When you observe, you look closely to pick out detail and to retain the information in your mind. You will probably be required to produce a developmental child study as part of your course. Observing babies and children is not easy and it is worth practising your observational skills before you begin.

Observational exercises

1. This is a simple 'spot the difference' game. See how many differences you can spot within five minutes (page 8 tells you how many there are).

Compare these two pictures – count the differences

2. Divide into four groups and place 20 familiar small objects on a tray; for example, a teaspoon, reel of cotton, cup, pencil, etc.
Group 1 Study the objects on the tray for one minute; remove the tray; write down all the objects you can remember; check your list.
Group 2 Study the objects on the tray for two minutes, then remove the tray and write out your list.
Group 3 study the objects on the tray for two minutes; remove the tray; write out your list half an hour later. Do not confer with the other groups.
Group 4 Study the tray of objects; after two minutes another person removes five of the objects and rearranges the remaining ones. The members of the group study the new arrangement for 30 seconds and then list the missing items.
Compare the results of each group's observations. What are your conclusions?

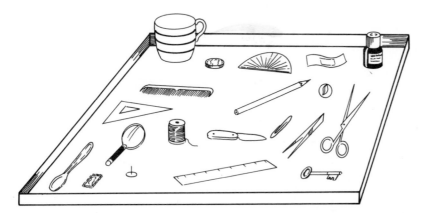

3. a) Study a colour picture of a baby for two minutes. Remove the picture and answer a set of preplanned questions; for example, was the child's hair straight or curly? What colour were the child's clothes? Were the child's eyes open or shut?
   b) Watch for two minutes a video of a child playing and then answer a set of preplanned questions similar to the ones above. Assess the results. Do you obtain more benefit from studying a static picture or a moving one? Which is it easier to study?

These exercises will show you:

● How good you are at observing.
● The skills needed for successful observation, for example, concentration, interest and accuracy.
● The importance of the time factor. The longer you observe, the more detail you retain; the longer the time lapse between observing and recording, the more likely you are to forget.
● The more practice you have at observing, the more skilful you will become.

General guidance

To get the maximum benefit from your observations you must plan and think carefully beforehand:

● What is the purpose of your observations? Are you studying a child at regular intervals over a short time (one week), or a long time (one year), to record his or her general development or a specific area of development; or are you studying several children to compare their stages of development and rates of progress?
● Will you need to take a chart or questionnaire to fill in as you observe? Remember how easy it is to forget details unless you record them straight away.

This is an example of the type of chart that can be filled in as observations are made:

Observation Chart: SOCIAL SKILLS Name: Date: Place: St Mark's Playgroup				
Questions	Amy 2 y 10 m	Bob 3 y 6 m	Roya 4 y 0 m	Leroy 4 y 7 m
Can the child: Put on his or her coat? Use a handkerchief? Visit the toilet unaided? Use a spoon? Use a beaker? Take off his or her shoes? Recognise his or her belongings?				
Code **** very well *** well ** poorly * not at all				
Conclusions				

Prepare your chart or questionnaire before you go on the visit. Set aside a specific time for making observations and make your observing inconspicuous. Many children show off if they know they are being watched.

● List the things you will need to take with you, for example, pencils, paper, charts, checklists, toy(s) for a child, clipboard and tape recorder.
● Have you got permission? You must not make detailed and recorded personal studies of children without permission from their parents, playgroup leaders, etc., before you begin. Explain what you are doing and why, and invite their

cooperation. Do your observing and recording with sensitivity. It will require interpersonal and caring skills.

- How will you collate and record your information? Consider all the possibilities shown in the following section and decide on the best one(s) for your particular piece of work.
- You can observe babies and children at a child clinic, council nursery, playgroup, nursery school, creche, mother and toddler group, play park, swimming pool, amusement park, pantomime or beach, or in shops or restaurants. Watch babies and children at different times of day, in different surroundings, with a variety of people and doing a variety of things.

Recording

Sometimes a written account is the best way of presenting your findings, but there are a number of other ways to record your results. Make your work interesting by using a variety of methods, selecting the method suitable for the information you are giving.

Surveys and market research are useful ways of collecting information. For example, you could do market research on mothers at a clinic:
Query – Do you use disposable nappies for your child?

No	Yes	Sometimes
JHT JHT JHT	JHT JHT I	JHT JHT JHT
JHT III		JHT JHT II
23	11	27

When you have analysed your findings there are numerous types of graph, chart, diagram, etc., which you can use to record your results, thus cutting down on the wordy and tedious explanations of many written reports.

Pictograms and pie charts

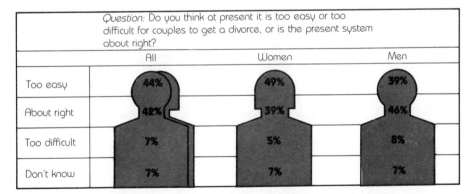

Question: Do you think at present it is too easy or too difficult for couples to get a divorce, or is the present system about right?

	All	Women	Men
Too easy	44%	49%	39%
About right	42%	39%	46%
Too difficult	7%	5%	8%
Don't know	7%	7%	7%

Five times as many seriously underweight babies are now surviving compared with ten years ago.

1976   1986

5

Fatal accidents

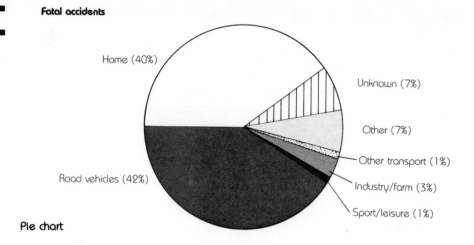

Home (40%)

Unknown (7%)

Other (7%)

Other transport (1%)

Industry/farm (3%)

Road vehicles (42%)

Sport/leisure (1%)

Pie chart

Graphs

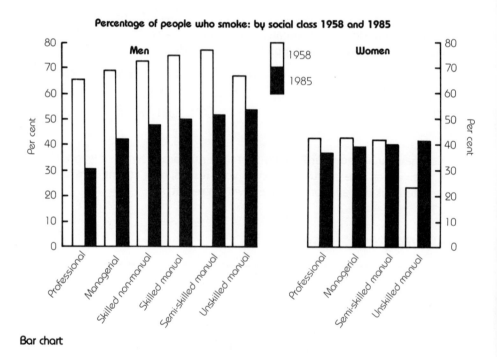

Percentage of people who smoke: by social class 1958 and 1985

Men

Women

1958

1985

Per cent

Per cent

Professional
Managerial
Skilled nonmanual
Skilled manual
Semi-skilled manual
Unskilled manual

Professional
Managerial
Semi-skilled manual
Unskilled manual

Bar chart

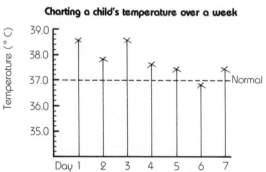

Charting a child's temperature over a week

Temperature (°C)

Normal

Day 1 2 3 4 5 6 7

Stick graph

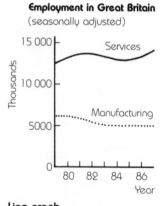

Employment in Great Britain
(seasonally adjusted)

Services

Thousands

Manufacturing

80 82 84 86

Year

Line graph

Maps, plans and diagrams

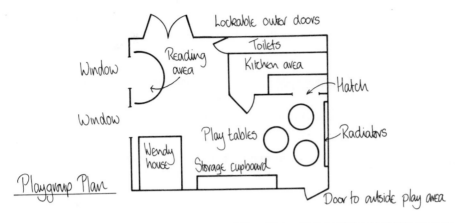

Playgroup Plan

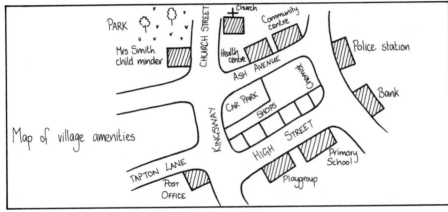

Map of village amenities

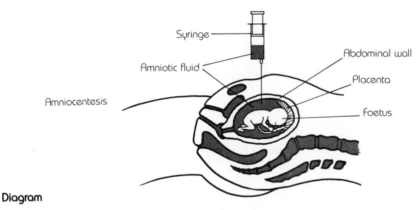

Diagram

Other suggestions for collecting and presenting your work appear throughout this book.

Methodology

A variety of ways of tackling your work (methodology) is used in this book:

● rounds   ● brainstorming   ● class and group discussions   ● collaborative learning games   ● role play and simulation   ● triggers   ● guest speakers   ● trails   ● visits   ● pre-coded questionnaires ●   class and individual surveys   ● fact files   ● investigations and experiments   ● case histories • community work • problem-solving assignments • posters and display work • quizzes and debates • syndicates • market research • varied group work.

Each working brief is clearly labelled with the methodology to be used.

Common elements and common themes

Child Development (Family) is one of the **four major aspects** of Home Economics. The others are: Home; Food; Textiles.

When Child Development is the **main study** the other three are known as the **common elements**.

All these aspects are interrelated and it is necessary to include all of them when studying this subject, and to include information from all the common elements in coursework and theory work.

All four major aspects are brought together by **seven common themes**. These are: 1. Human development 2. Health 3. Safety and protection 4. Efficiency 5. Values 6. Aesthetics 7. Interaction with the environment.

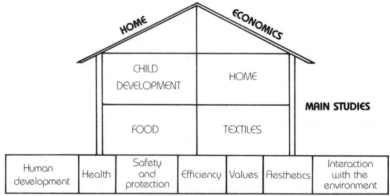

These seven themes form the essential bases for all four aspects of study. The link-up charts at the end of the book show clearly these interrelationships.

Answer to spot the difference game (pages 2 and 3) There are 11 differences.

UNIT ONE

Responsibilities for Parenthood

Study Area 1

Core information

Preconceptual care and planning

Preconceptual care involves making plans and preparations before starting a family. Every baby should be a wanted baby, and modern methods of contraception allow couples to plan the size of their families and choose when to start them. Pregnancy should be a pleasurable time for both parents, not a time for stress, fear, worry, overwork and poor health.

Ideally children need:
● parents who have a stable, loving relationship and a mature outlook ● the security of a warm, comfortable home ● adequate and nourishing food ● a clean and safe environment.

Before starting a family, a couple should consider these needs.

Many children are brought up in poor conditions with such problems as:
● overcrowding ● poor sanitation ● inadequate heating ● vermin infestation ● dirty, vandalised buildings ● unsafe buildings ● no play areas ● homelessness or inadequate temporary accommodation.

Parents must also consider their finances. It is estimated that the cost of bringing up a child until the age of sixteen is more than £30 000:

feeding, clothing, heating for a child under 5 = £28.07 per week

feeding, clothing, heating for a child 5–11 = £38.99 per week

feeding, clothing, heating for a child 12–16 = £56.21 per week

Parents must consider their family roles. Many years ago women were not expected to work outside the home when they married, but nowadays women and men are educated to the same level, there is legislation for equal job opportunities and most fathers help with child rearing. The average age of all mothers at childbirth has increased steadily since the mid 1970s and in 1985 was 27 years.

Planning ahead

The key factor in producing a healthy baby is the health of the prospective parents. An unhealthy couple may find it difficult to conceive. A man's sperm is affected by the state of his health and a woman must be healthy in order to support the foetus in the womb from the moment of conception.

Couples planning to start a family should consider:
- diet   • environment   • use of body pollutants such as tobacco
- disease   • levels of stress.

Diet

All food provides us with energy. Energy not used by the body will be stored as fat and make us overweight. The number of calories an individual needs per day depends upon:
- state of health   • age   • active or non-active occupation   • gender (male or female)   • climate   • metabolism.

> Average daily calorie (kcal) needs for a woman = 2000–2500
>
> Average daily calorie (kcal) needs for a man = 2500–3000

Anyone who is severely overweight (obese):

• cannot get about easily   • puts strain on the legs, thus encouraging varicose veins and muscular pains   • risks developing high blood pressure, gallstones and heart disease   • is more likely to have accidents   • may develop chest complaints   • may have complications after operations   • women may have complications during pregnancy.

Slimming is not the answer to obesity. As soon as you go back to a previous pattern of eating, the fat returns. To maintain a good shape and feel fit and healthy:
- Decide the correct weight for your height.
- Stick to a sensible eating plan.
- Keep in trim with suitable exercise.

Use the chart below as a guide to your weight, but do not become obsessed with weighing yourself. It is normal for body weight to change frequently for many reasons.

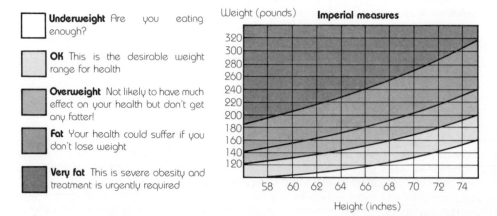

Underweight Are you eating enough?

OK This is the desirable weight range for health

Overweight Not likely to have much effect on your health but don't get any fatter!

Fat Your health could suffer if you don't lose weight

Very fat This is severe obesity and treatment is urgently required

Chart of women's weight

Practical Health magazine

HIGH FIBRE
LOW FAT
NO ARTIFICIAL ADDITIVES

BEANS in tomato sauce
447 gram 15¾ oz
REDUCED SUGAR, REDUCED SALT
■ HIGH FIBRE

H I G H
F I B R E

NO ARTIFICIAL PRESERVATIVES COLOURS OR FLAVOURING
NO ADDED SUGAR

TYPICAL NUTRITIONAL COMPOSITION PER 100 GRAMMES	
Energy	1385 kJ
	325 kcal
Protein (N x 5.7)	9.0 g
Fat	1.2 g
Dietary Fibre	6.1 g
Available Carbohydrate	74.2 g
Vitamins:	
Niacin	16.0 mg
Vitamin B$_6$	1.8 mg
Riboflavin (B$_2$)	1.5 mg
Thiamin (B$_1$)	1.0 mg
Folic Acid	250 µg
Vitamin D	2.8 µg
Vitamin B$_{12}$	1.7 µg
Iron	6.7 mg

CALORIES PER BAR. 117		
TYPICAL NUTRITIONAL CONTENT PER 100g		
ENERGY	1465 kJ/350 kcal	
PROTEIN		6.3 g
OIL.		14 g
of which:	TOTAL	6.3 g
	SATURATES	7.7 g
	UNSATURATES	
AVAILABLE CARBOHYDRATE		51 g
DIETARY FIBRE		14 g

Nutrition guides on food packaging

Food is made up of **nutrients**. A healthy diet includes proteins, carbohydrates, fats, vitamins, minerals, fibre and fluids.

No one food contains all the nutrients. Therefore a correct diet must be **varied** and **balanced**. Follow the National Advisory Committee on Nutrition Education (NACNE) report advice:

- Have **less** fat, **less** sugar, **less** salt, **more** fibre.
- Eat moderate amounts of a varied diet. Cut out snacks and have smaller helpings.
- Drink plenty of water and fresh fruit juice. Use decaffeinated coffee. Try herbal and lemon teas. Remember alcoholic drinks are high in calories.
- Choose fresh foods rather than convenience foods. Avoid foods high in additives and high in fat. Choose take-away meals carefully.
- Read and understand the labels on foods.

Enjoy your food and don't feel guilty if you break your healthy eating plan with the occasional chocolate bar.

Fruit juice   Yoghurt   Banana

Steamed pudding

Fizzy drink   Custard

Jacket potato   Omelette
Peas   Tomato

A healthy meal

Fatty pork chop
Chips   Peas

A not so healthy meal

To reinforce a healthy diet, regular, sensible **exercise** will:
- use up surplus energy
- keep the figure trim
- tone the muscles
- increase stamina and suppleness
- make you feel better.

Cycling, walking, swimming, dancing and gardening are all good forms of exercise. If your daily routine involves a lot of sitting try to take regular exercise. This may help with any sleep problems.

Environment

A child's environment will affect his or her physical, intellectual and social development; therefore a couple who are planning a family should try if possible, to live in:

- A **healthy** environment
  Air which is polluted by factory waste, petrol fumes, smoke and damp can cause chest complaints, rheumatic diseases and conditions related to lead poisoning. A developing foetus can be badly affected by polluted air.
  Tap water is usually fit to drink in the UK, but water in ponds, rivers and the sea is often polluted by factory waste, dead animals or sewage.
  The **land** we live on may be polluted by all types of rubbish, animal faeces or agricultural chemicals. Rural areas are usually healthier than the more densely populated towns.

- A **safe** environment
  Accidents can happen anywhere but they are more likely in areas of heavy traffic, dense population and badly planned housing. They may occur in shops, play areas or badly lit places. Pregnancy can be a particularly hazardous time, unless the expectant mother is especially safety conscious. If possible houses should be chosen with accident prevention in mind – away from water, steep slopes and heavy traffic.

- A **relaxing** environment
  Modern living conditions put people under various sorts of pressure – noise, overcrowding, problems at school or work, financial and social. A build-up of pressure will result in stress, which can cause depression, sleep problems and stress-related illnesses.

- A **stimulating** environment
  Children need external stimulation if they are to develop to their full potential. Intending parents should ideally look for an environment which offers:

  - good educational facilities
  - opportunities for social contact
  - good community facilities such as health centres and mother and baby groups
  - sports facilities such as a swimming pool, adventure playground or leisure centre.

Body pollutants

It has been proved that body pollutants will harm not only the health of the parents but also the life of the unborn child. Tobacco, alcohol and drugs taken in excess can cause:

- habits which are hard to break
- reduced resistance to disease
- severe emotional and mental changes
- infertility
- social and marital problems
- financial hardship
- chronic or acute illness, which may lead to death.

Smoking A woman who is planning a pregnancy or who is pregnant must try not to smoke for the sake of her own and the baby's health. Smoking during pregnancy may cause:

- an undernourished foetus
- low birth-weight and premature babies
- higher neonatal death rate.
- congenital abnormalities in the foetus
- spontaneous abortion

Passive smoking (absorbing fumes when someone else is smoking) puts a child's health at risk, so the rest of the family should not smoke either.

Alcohol during pregnancy can contribute to the foetus having:
- facial abnormalities such as cleft palate
- heart defects
- abnormal limb development
- poor developmental progress resulting in lower intelligence.

Children are often severely emotionally affected if they have alcoholic parents.

Drugs Anyone who is a drug addict must get medical help before starting a pregnancy. Any type of drug can cause damage to a foetus, such as:
- congenital malformations
- low birth weight
- retarded intellectual development
- when born the baby may be addicted.

Not even over-the-counter drugs should be taken without consulting a doctor. Women who take drugs prescribed for a medical condition such as diabetes must discuss the situation with their doctor before conception.

Disease and infections

Some conditions, such as viral infections, can pass through the placenta to the foetus and cause damage.

The most common viral infection (apart from the common cold) is rubella (German measles) which can cause a baby to be born blind, deaf or physically deformed if the mother is exposed to the disease in the early months of pregnancy. Influenza, mumps and chicken pox can also damage the foetus.

Vaccination for such diseases should not be given during pregnancy. A woman who is planning a pregnancy should check her immunity, and if she needs a vaccination against rubella she should then wait three months before conceiving.

Sexually transmitted diseases (STDs) may affect the ability to conceive. Certain STDs, including AIDS, can seriously affect a developing foetus and the baby may be born with the disease. Treatment and advice must be taken before conception takes place if either partner suspects an infection.

Some diseases or malformations are inherited – they pass from generation to generation. Within the nucleus of the cells which make up the human body are chromosomes, and in each chromosome are genes which are responsible for the transmission of hereditary characteristics. There are 23 pairs of chromosomes in each cell, including two sex chromosomes.

An abnormality in the number of chromosomes in a cell can result in a condition such as Down's Syndrome, which occurs when an extra chromosome is present. Some abnormalities are passed on by one or both parents, though they themselves may be normal. These inherited conditions include phenylketonuria (PKU), cystic fibrosis and galactosaemia. Some 'sex-linked' conditions such as haemophilia are usually only passed on from the mother, who is the carrier, to the son.

It is possible to reduce the risks of having a deformed or infected child by taking advice, tests and treatments before, or during, pregnancy. Partners who think they may have an abnormality or disease which could be passed on to their child should consult their GP or family planning clinic for advice and tests.

X-rays during pregnancy can damage the foetus.

Pupil participation

Working briefs

1. Relationships   Individual work (Questionnaire)

Below is a set of personal questions which a couple who are undecided about starting a family could consider. What impression would the responses on the right give you? Would you consider that a couple giving these replies was ready for parenthood?

Questions	Responses
Do you think that a couple should be married before having children?	Doesn't matter.
How long have you lived together/been married?	Six months.
Do you consider your relationship to be a permanent one?	Don't know.
Have you both got similar interests?	Yes.
Would it worry you to have to stay in nearly every evening?	Yes.
Do you have an active social life?	Yes.
Would you be happy to let your partner have evenings out every week with friends?	Yes – if I could too.
Do you think that a baby can be reared happily and healthily in a caravan/bed-sit/high rise flat/living with in-laws?	Why not?
Why do you want to have a baby?	Babies are so lovely.

Which word from each of the pairs below would you choose to describe this couple?

reliable/unreliable   mature/immature   selfish/unselfish
responsible/irresponsible   sensitive/insensitive

Give reasons for your answers. Write down another set of responses which would give a different impression.

2. Divorce   Group discussion

Discuss the following aspects of divorce in small groups. Elect a group leader to summarise the points raised in your discussion group. A final class discussion will bring together all the issues.

a) 'Divorce is too easy to obtain.'
b) The possible effects upon the children of their parents' divorce.
c) Relationships within the family after a divorce has been finalised.
d) Ways in which a marriage may be mended.

(See example on page 53.)

3. Finance

Budgeting Paul is a telephone fitter and earns £180 per week; less tax and National Insurance payments = £135 per week. His wife, Jenny, is a nurse and earns £120 per week; less tax and National Insurance payments = £95 per week.

They have a mortgage costing   £35 per week
          community charge is   £10 per week

Pupil 1. Plan the weekly budget for this couple when they are both earning.
Pupil 2. Plan the weekly budget if Jenny stops going out to work.
Together. Show how savings can be made in transport, fuel, clothing, food, etc.

4. Diet

Situation: Emma and Ben, a young, active, married couple, are slightly overweight and do not have a healthy diet. They eat too much saturated fat and refined carbohydrates and not enough fibre.

Assignment A These are typical meals which they may eat on any Saturday. Suggest how these meals could be replanned to provide a healthier diet.

Breakfast	Snack	Lunch (bought out)	Tea	Evening meal

| Fried bacon sandwich | Coffee and doughnut | Pizza and chips | Mug of tea
Cake
Scone and jam | Meat pie
Carrots
Sauté potatoes
Gravy
Cream meringue |

Assignment B Emma and Ben eat too many convenience foods, such as packet soups, complete frozen meals, etc., because they are too tired to cook an elaborate meal after a day's work.

Plan and cook a two-course meal which would only take about 30 minutes to prepare and cook. Use as few convenience foods as possible.

Example. First course: Chicken and beansprout stir-fry.
Ingredients: 150 g (6 oz) raw chicken cut into thin strips coated with seasoned flour, florets of cauliflower, $\frac{1}{2}$ red pepper, 2 carrots cut into thin strips, 3 chopped spring onions, 100 g (4 oz) bean sprouts, 1 tbsp corn oil, 1 clove of garlic or a small piece of chopped, fresh ginger.
Method: Heat the oil, cook the chicken, garlic and/or ginger for 2 min. Add the vegetables (these may be quickly blanched for 2 min if wished). Add 1 tbsp soy sauce and 1 tbsp sherry or water. Cook 1–2 min. Add the beansprouts and heat through.

Second course: Banana bake.
Method: Put two bananas in an oven-proof dish, add 2 tbsps orange or lemon juice, 1 tbsp honey or brown sugar, 1 oz polyunsaturated margarine. Cover with foil. Bake in the oven at 200°C or gas Mark 5 for 15 min, or in the microwave oven for 4 min (replacing foil with cling film for the microwave). Serve with plain yoghurt.

Time your work exactly and estimate how it could be reduced by preparing some things before leaving for work in the morning.

5. Diet

YOUR DAY'S EATING PATTERN

(Department of Health recommendations)

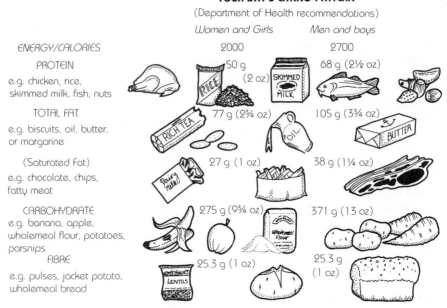

	Women and Girls	Men and boys
ENERGY/CALORIES	2000	2700
PROTEIN e.g. chicken, rice, skimmed milk, fish, nuts	50 g (2 oz)	68 g (2½ oz)
TOTAL FAT e.g. biscuits, oil, butter, or margarine	77 g (2¾ oz)	105 g (3¾ oz)
(Saturated fat) e.g. chocolate, chips, fatty meat	27 g (1 oz)	38 g (1¼ oz)
CARBOHYDRATE e.g. banana, apple, wholemeal flour, potatoes, parsnips	275 g (9¾ oz)	371 g (13 oz)
FIBRE e.g. pulses, jacket potato, wholemeal bread	25.3 g (1 oz)	25.3 g (1 oz)

Keep a diary for a week showing all the food which you eat. Don't forget the snacks!

At the end of the week evaluate your diet. Is it a healthy diet?

Are you eating too much sugar, fat, salt and not enough fibre? If so, how can you adapt your diet?

Are you overweight? Use the chart on page 10 as a guide. Your normal energy intake should be approximately:

> girls – 2000 kcals per day   boys – 2500 kcals per day

How could you sensibly cut down your calorie intake to reduce your weight gradually?

(See example on page 53.)

6. Environment

Carry out a survey of your local environment. Note the places which quickly become dirty and untidy, such as bus shelters, areas near take-away food shops, etc. Why these places? Are there any corners, alleyways, etc., where rubbish tends to pile up? Why?

Note the litter bins. How far apart are they? Are they used? Are they efficiently designed? How often are they emptied? Is there much fouling of the area by dogs or other animals? Check the by-laws relating to this.

Check your recreation grounds. Are they untidy and covered with litter? How often are the dustbins emptied in your area? How often does street cleaning take place and is it efficient?

Assess your results: how can people be encouraged to consider their environment? How could improvements be made in your area? What are the dangers from pollution? Contact your local council to find out what they are doing about maintaining a healthy environment. Finally, discuss your findings in class. It would be helpful if a member of your local council or area environmental office could join you.

7. Body pollutants

Tobacco　　　　　　　　　　　　　　**Individual work (Investigation)**

Situation: Margot smokes 15 cigarettes a day.
　　　　　　Clive smokes 20 cigarettes a day.
How much, approximately, do they spend on cigarettes per week?

Margot would like to buy a new dress and a handbag. Clive would like to buy a leather jacket and a camera. They would both like to buy a washing machine and an electric toaster.
For how long would they have to give up smoking to buy these things?
Compile a booklet giving a selection of tips on the best ways of giving up smoking.

Alcohol　　　　　　　　　　　　　　**Class work (Fact file)**

Make a fact file of newspaper cuttings showing the types of offences committed by people under the influence of alcohol, ranging from driving offences to assault. Notice the ages of the offenders.
'Drunkenness amongst young people is increasing because . . .' Take one minute to think about this and then go round the class quickly completing the sentence. Assess the results of your research.

Drugs　　　　　　　　　　　　　**Class work (Guest speaker)**

Invite someone from your local police/drugs squad to talk to you about the use of illegal drugs. The speaker may be able to show a film or slides and discuss case histories.

Preliminary preparations: Decide who will contact the speaker, who will look after him or her and who will plan the venue, video equipment, etc.

The group should plan a series of questions to ask the speaker; for example, what are the differences between soft and hard drugs? Why are illegal drugs bad for us? A follow-on debriefing session should be held to help with any points not understood.

8. Chromosomes and genes　　　Class work (Triggers)

a) As many pupils as possible should bring a photograph of a person in their family whom they resemble. Mix up the photographs, place them on a table and let everyone see whether they can identify the relationships.
b) Draw up a personal profile of characteristics. Check how many of them 'run in the family'. Become aware of family resemblances; for example, blue eyes, facial shape, plump ankles, red hair, quick temper, etc.

　　Relate these 'triggers' to information on chromosomes and genes. Do some research into inherited diseases such as PKU or haemophilia.

　　(See example on page 54.)

9. Stress　　　　　　　　Individual work (Investigation)

Stress symptoms

Find out how and why the following procedures help to relieve anxiety and stress: setting aside a time for relaxation; joining a keep fit class; learning relaxation exercises; breathing in and out deeply; learning yoga; cutting down on tea, coffee and coke; finding someone who will listen to your problems; reassessing your diet; taking up regular exercise; giving up some responsibilities; not leaving everything until the last minute.

The list shown here details many of the signs which indicate the stress syndrome. Three or four 'yeses' mean that the situation should be tackled straight away. Try the test on yourself (although young people are not usually over-stressed) and try it on an adult whom you know well and who will not mind answering the questions.

	YES	NO
Have you developed any new nervous habits – i.e., nail biting, fidgeting, continually touching your hair or face?		
Are you drinking, smoking or 'comfort eating' more?		
Has your sleep pattern changed?		
Are you getting digestive upsets?		
Are you suffering headaches, breathlessness, even fainting or crying spells?		
Do you feel under such pressure that you can't finish one job properly before dashing on to the next?		
Do you feel irritable, or have a 'hair-trigger' temper?		
Is it hard to make decisions?		
Is it difficult to concentrate because your mind is racing?		
Is your memory getting worse?		
Is your confidence and self-esteem slipping?		
Do you feel constantly guilty?		
Do you dread the future?		
Are you hyperactive physically?		
Have you lost interest in life?		

Practical Health magazine

Written work

Fact finding exercise

Use one sentence to explain each of the following terms:

dependent children   parental roles   status   body pollutants
metabolism   role reversal   nutrients   NACNE   colour
coding   neonatal death rate   passive smoking.

What is the difference between:

manual and non-manual work?   obesity and undernourishment?
a rural and an urban environment?   chronic and acute illnesses?

Find out about and write notes on:

the effects of lead poisoning   stress-related illnesses   environmental
pollution and the Clean Air Acts   diseases contracted from animals.

Application of knowledge

Write a paragraph about:

Some aspects of a healthy lifestyle.
The possible physical and emotional effects of obesity.
A balanced and varied diet.
The use of convenience foods and fast-food shops.
Safety features in a family home.

Free response

1.   Plan a three month count-down of preconceptual care for a couple who are hoping to start a family. Give reasons for your suggestions.

2. In recent years it has been realised that there is much parents can do to ensure a healthy pregnancy and a healthy baby before conception takes place. Explain how, with good preconceptual care and sensible planning, a couple can help to ensure this.

MEG Child Development examination question, 1986

Data response

United Kingdom	1965	1985
Population	54.3 million	56.6 million
Number of marriages	422 000	393 000
Number of children born	1 million	750 000
Infant mortality rate	19.6%	9.4%
Number of divorces	41 000	175 000

Central Statistical Office

		Marks
1.	a) How many years do these figures span?	1
	b) By how many has the population increased?	1
2.	a) Is the birth rate decreasing or increasing?	1
	b) Suggest two reasons for this.	2
3.	a) Are the divorce figures two, three or four times higher in 1985 than in 1965?	1
	b) Suggest three reasons for the increase in divorce.	6
4.	a) Explain the term 'infant mortality rate'.	2
	b) Give four ways in which prospective parents can plan for a healthy child.	4
5.	Marriages still take place in approximately the same numbers as 20 years ago, and there are also other forms of permanent relationships. Explain some of the benefits of a stable partnership.	7
		25

Self-assessment

Photocopy and complete the self-assessment chart on page 161, inserting the following list of topics under 'The work I have done includes':

1. Relationships
2. Finance
3. Diet
4. Environment
5. Smoking
6. Alcohol
7. Drug abuse
8. Disease and infections
9. Stress.

Photocopy and complete the self-marking plan on page 162 for the eight working briefs in this unit.

UNIT TWO

Biological Background

Core information

The reproductive system

The three main jobs of the reproductive system are:

- For the female to produce eggs (ova) and the male to produce sperm.
- For the sperm to fertilise the egg and conception to take place.
- To provide nourishment for the resulting embryo and a place for it to develop.

Female Organs	Functions	Male Organs	Functions
Ovaries	Produce and release eggs (ovulation); control the female sex hormones.	Testes	Located in the scrotum, they produce sperm and the male sex hormone.
Fallopian tubes (oviducts)	Join the ovaries to the womb; site of fertilisation.	Sperm ducts (vas deferens)	Tubes leading from the testes, along which the sperm travels.
Uterus (womb)	Pear-shaped organ which houses the developing baby.	Seminal vesicles	Glands which produce the fluid which carries the sperm (semen).
Cervix	The lower end or neck of the womb.	Urethra	A tube which runs from the bladder and seminal vesicles down the centre of the penis and which carries urine or semen.
Vagina	A tube 10–12 cm (4–5 in) long, leading from the cervix to the surface of the body.	Penis	An organ made from spongy tissue which hardens and becomes erect during intercourse.
Vulva	The area where the vaginal opening is situated.		

Puberty

Puberty is the stage at which:

- sex hormones start to develop and are released
- sperm or ova begin to be produced.

Puberty usually begins when a child is between eleven and fourteen years old.

These physical changes take place at puberty:

Male sex hormone testosterone stimulates:
Growth of pubic hair and hair on face and chest.
Muscular development.
Deepening voice.
Growth of sex organs.

 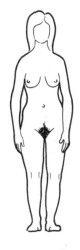

Female sex hormones oestrogen and progesterone stimulate:
Start of menstruation.
Growth of pubic and under-arm hair.
Development of breasts and nipples.
Fat deposits on hips.

Menstruation

Menstruation (having periods) is a regular, female, monthly cycle which starts at puberty.

Days 1–5   The lining of the womb is shed as a menstrual flow (bleeding).
Days 6–12   Menstruation ceases.
Days 13–15 The most fertile period. Ovulation (the release of an egg) takes place in the middle of the cycle.
Day 21   A fertilised egg will reach the uterus about this time.
Day 29   If the egg has not been fertilised the cycle will repeat itself with the start of a period.

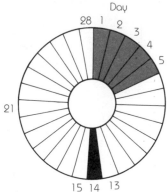

Menstrual Period

Ovulation

Typical 28–day cycle

Variations
The cycle may be irregular if the woman is under stress. Flow may be scanty or dry up altogether if she is severely undernourished. Heavy periods may result from a physical abnormality. Taking the contraceptive pill may regulate the cycle or make the flow scanty.

Problems
Period pains – including cramps and sickness, premenstrual syndrome (PMS) – headache, sickness, irritability and emotional upset. Body odour may be increased so personal hygiene is essential. Fatigue during a period is common: iron rich foods, rest and sensible exercise are needed for this.

Menstruation will cease during the menopause, which occurs between the ages of 45 and 55.

Fertilisation and conception

During sexual intercourse the penis is inserted into the vagina and sperm are ejected from the penis into the vagina. Fertilisation takes place in the oviduct when a sperm penetrates the egg. Sperm and egg cells are called 'sex cells' or **gametes**. They each contain 23 chromosomes.

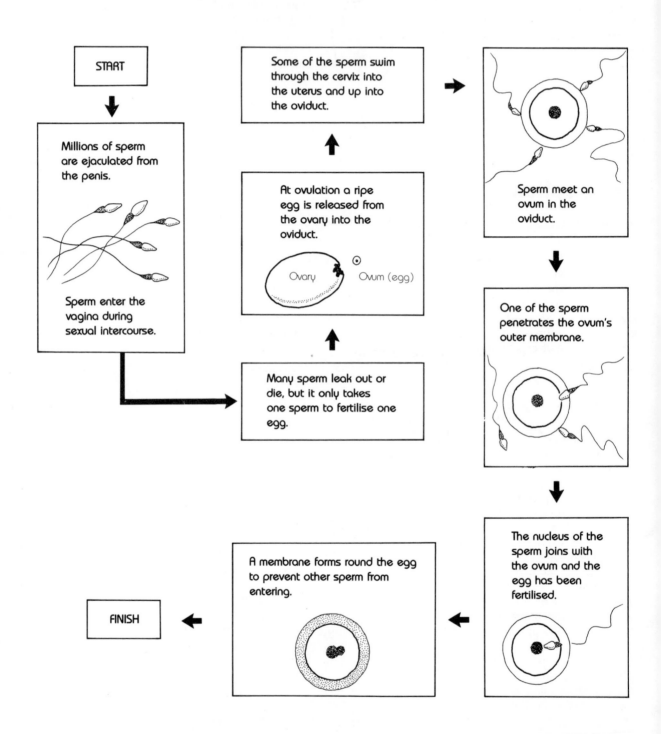

The fertilised egg has 46 chromosomes, 23 from each partner. After fertilisation the fertilised egg (**zygote**) travels down the Fallopian tube (**oviduct**). From fertilisation to implantation takes about a week:

Day 1. Fertilisation occurs.
Day 2. The fertilised egg travels along the Fallopian tube, dividing and sub-dividing into the cells which make an **embryo**.
Day 4. The embryo, a hollow ball of cells, reaches the uterus. This is the **blastocyst** stage.
Day 7. The embryo attaches itself to the thickened lining of the uterus. This is **implantation**.

The outer layer of cells burrows into the lining and forms the **placenta**; the inner layer of cells will develop into the baby.

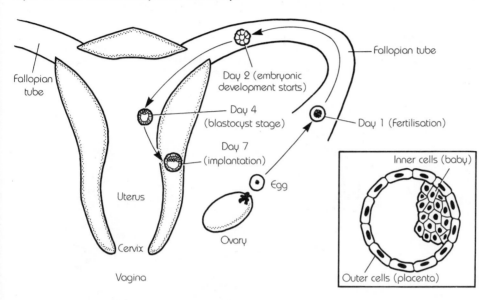

The placenta and developing embryo are connected by the **umbilical cord**. As it grows the embryo will be enclosed in a bag of liquid called the **amniotic sac**, filled with **amniotic fluid**.

The Placenta	The Amniotic Sac
● Provides food for the developing embryo. Passes nutrients from the mother's blood into the baby's blood stream. ● Transfers oxygen from the mother to the embryo and carries away carbon dioxide. ● Removes waste products in the form of urea. ● Prevents some harmful germs and drugs passing from mother to embryo. ● Produces and releases pregnancy hormones.	● Is composed of two thin layers of tissue, an outer layer, the **chorion** and an inner layer, the **amnion**. ● Provides a muscular bag of fluid in which the embryo develops. ● Maintains a constant temperature. ● Protects the embryo from shocks and knocks. ● Gives the embryo freedom of movement. ● Helps to prevent infection.
The Umbilical Cord	**The Amniotic Fluid**
● Links the embryo to the placenta. ● Supports two arteries and a vein which transfer blood to and from the embryo. ● The cord and the placenta are expelled as afterbirth when the baby is born.	● Is made up of water, salts, fats and foetal urine. At 10 weeks there is about 100 ml ($3\frac{1}{2}$ oz) of fluid, at 40 weeks about 2000 ml ($3\frac{1}{2}$ pts). ● Absorbs the foetal waste. ● Is the medium in which the foetus learns to swallow and breathe.

Foetal development

A normal pregnancy lasts nine months, or 40 weeks, or 266 days from conception (280 days from the first day of the last period).

Signs of pregnancy

- a missed period   ● nausea (from about the sixth week)   ● enlarged and tender breasts   ● a need to pass urine more frequently   ● tiredness
- steady weight gain (average 1 kg ($2\frac{1}{4}$ lb) in the first twelve weeks).

Pregnancy tests

These may take the form of urine tests, either carried out by a doctor or a home kit for self-testing, or an internal examination by a doctor.

Stages of foetal growth

FIVE WEEKS
The embryo is the size of a little fingernail. The heart is formed and there are limb buds. The eyes are recognisable.

SEVEN WEEKS
Muscles and bones are beginning to develop. The embryo at twelve weeks is called a foetus.

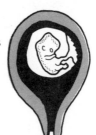

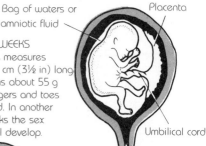

Bag of waters or amniotic fluid

Placenta

THIRTEEN WEEKS
The foetus measures about 8–9 cm (3½ in) long, and weighs about 55 g (2 oz). Fingers and toes are formed. In another three weeks the sex organs will develop.

Umbilical cord

Cervix or neck of womb

20 WEEKS
The foetus weighs 280 g (10 oz) and is 20 cm (8 in) long. Eyebrows are growing and the heart beat can be heard.

28 WEEKS (SIX MONTHS)

SEVEN MONTHS
Already in position for birth. In the next two months the foetus will grow bigger still until ready to be born. The cord provides nourishment from the placenta.

40 WEEKS (NINE MONTHS)

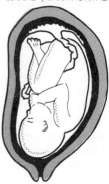

Multiple pregnancies

- One in 99 pregnancies results in twins.
  One in 6000 pregnancies results in triplets.
  One in 500 000 pregnancies results in quadruplets.

- There are two types of twins:
  Identical (uniovular) twins develop from a single egg fertilised by a single sperm. They share the same placenta, are the same sex and look alike.
  Non-identical twins (binovular) develop from two eggs which are fertilised by two sperm. They have different placenta, may be of different sexes and are three times more common than identical twins.

- The tendency towards a multiple pregnancy often runs in the family.
- They are more frequent in women with large numbers of children already.
- They are more likely to occur in older women.
- They are usually diagnosed at the first ultra-sound examination.
- Twins are often born early and small for the expected dates.
- A multiple birth may cause complications; therefore, it is usual to have a hospital delivery.

Pupil participation

Working briefs

1. Menstruation
Group discussion

Divide into small groups to discuss these aspects of menstruation:

a) Exercise and diet during menstruation.
b) Emotional upsets and their effects during this time.
c) Personal hygiene during menstruation.
d) Physical problems of menstruation, such as period pains.

You may need to do some research into your topic. Summarise your findings with the rest of the class and then draw up a ten-point guidance plan to help during menstruation.

2. Menstruation
Problem-solving assignment

Put together a simple, mainly pictorial booklet which would explain puberty and menstruation to a child. Remember, periods can start as early as nine or ten years old and the experience can be frightening to a child who is unaware of the cause. The booklet could also be useful for slow-learning children.

(See example on page 54.)

3. Reproductive organs
Individual work
(Collaborative learning game)

You must remember the correct biological diagrams, the names of the organs and their correct spelling. As a memory aid, assemble and label the pieces shown below. You could produce your own jigsaw and keep it in your information file.

Do a similar piece of work for the male reproductive organs.

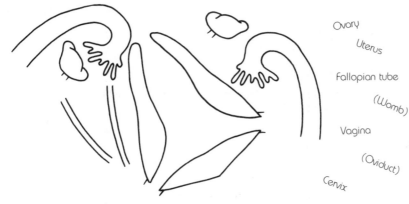

Ovary

Uterus

Fallopian tube

(Womb)

Vagina

(Oviduct)

Cervix

Female reproductive organs

4. Foetal development

Individual work
(Display work/fact file)

Produce a wallchart or frieze to show how the foetus develops from week one to week 40. Collect pictures or copy them from magazines, leaflets, etc., to illustrate each stage and describe the changes which take place.

Did you know that:

- The developing foetus reacts to bright lights and loud noises outside the uterus?
- A foetus may suck its thumb for comfort?

Find out more facts like this and produce a fact file for an expectant mother or father.

5. Pregnancy

Class work (Guest speaker)

Invite a member of the National Childbirth Trust (NCT) to one of your lessons to discuss aspects of pregnancy and birth with you. The NCT exists to educate people for parenthood. You can find information about it from the public library, or the NCT headquarters.

Get to know some facts about the NCT and prepare a series of trigger points to start your interview; for example:

- Would you please describe the work of the NCT?
- How did the organisation start?
- Why is it important to train young people for parenthood?
- What is meant by natural childbirth and why would you recommend it?
- Can you recommend any information leaflets or booklets to help us?

Don't forget to appoint someone to welcome your speaker, to provide a cup of tea and to thank him or her afterwards.

6. Multiple pregnancies

Class work
(Pre-coded questionnaire/survey)

Survey your school and nearby primary schools to discover the numbers of twins, triplets and quads who attend. What is the total number of pupils in each school? Use a pre-coded questionnaire to determine facts such as the sex of the twins, their ethnic group, whether they are identical or non-identical, whether there is more than one set of twins in the family. Collate your results to discover what proportion of the children you have surveyed is the result of multiple pregnancies and how this compares with the figures on page 24.

(See example on page 55.)

Written work

Fact finding exercise

Find out and explain the meaning of the following terms which are connected with puberty and menstruation:

dysmenorrhoea   PMS   pituitary gland   ovulation.

Compare the work of:

The testes and the ovaries.
The sperm ducts and the Fallopian tubes.
The uterus and the placenta.

Short answer questions

1. Why does menstruation always cease during pregnancy?

2. What is the average length of   a) the menstrual cycle
   b) a normal pregnancy?

3. Name one male and one female sex hormone.

4. Name two female organs which only develop during pregnancy.

5. Describe the journey of the egg from its release from the ovary through fertilisation to implantation.

6. Give two of the functions of the placenta and two functions of the amniotic sac during pregnancy.

7. What is an embryo and when does it become a foetus?

8. Describe the embryo/foetus at: the five-week stage; 12-week stage; 28-week stage; 40-week stage.

9. Compare the different ways in which identical and non-identical twins are formed.

10. What are Siamese twins and of what are they the result?

Free response questions

Puberty and menstruation bring about not only physical, but also emotional changes. Discuss the form these emotional changes take, their effects and what can be done to help the emotional problems of puberty.

Self-assessment ————————————

Photocopy and complete the self-assessment chart on page 161, inserting the following list of topics under 'The work I have done includes':

1. Reproduction
2. Puberty
3. Menstruation
4. Fertilisation
5. Conception
6. Foetal development
7. Multiple pregnancies.

Photocopy and complete the self-marking plans on page 162 for the six working briefs in this unit.

Study Area **1**

Pregnancy

Core Information

Antenatal care

Some reasons for care during pregnancy are:

- To ensure that the pregnant woman remains as healthy as possible during her pregnancy and produces a healthy baby.
- To monitor the progress of the developing foetus and spot any abnormalities at an early stage so that treatment can be given.
- To give counselling to those women who are at risk of producing a deformed child.
- To give special care to those women who are in high risk groups.

Women at special risk during pregnancy are those who:

- have three or more children   ● have a poor obstetric history   ● have a multiple pregnancy   ● are under 16 or over 35   ● have a small pelvic area   ● are much overweight   ● are heavy smokers or heavy drinkers   ● live in conditions of poor housing, or with insufficient food.

Infant mortality rate These figures show the deaths of infants under one year per 1000 live births recorded in 1985:

Italy	10.9	The rate tends to be lower in countries
UK	9.4	which have a high proportion of skilled
Switzerland	7.6	medical people, a high standard of living
Japan	6.0	and good antenatal care facilities.

Encyclopaedia Britannica

Here are some of the ways in which the pregnant woman can help herself during pregnancy:

Diet

DO

- Have a carefully balanced diet with plenty of foods containing protein, vitamins, calcium and iron and plenty of fluids.

- Take food a little and often.

- Use fresh foods as opposed to processed foods from which nutrients may have been lost.

- Find out the foods which suit her and avoid those which are hard to digest, such as highly spiced or acidic foods.

- Eat sufficient to satisfy hunger, but avoid putting on too much weight. The chart opposite shows an acceptable level of weight gain.

DON'T

- Have a lot of snacks which have little nutritional value, such as crisps.

- Have a lot of fatty foods which are difficult to digest.

- Have a lot of foods which contain high levels of added chemicals.

- Have drinks with high caffeine content, such as coffee or colas.

- Take much sweet food and drinks, such as lemonade, cakes and biscuits, which contain a lot of 'empty calories'.

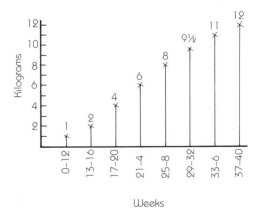

Typical weight gain of a pregnant woman

Clothing

DO	DON'T
• Choose clothing which is inexpensive, cheerful and well designed.	• Buy garments which restrict the developing figure or restrict movement.
• Go for natural fibres which are absorbent and comfortable.	• Choose garments which are difficult to launder, need a lot of ironing or expensive dry cleaning.
• Consider safety – garments which are too tight, over fussy, too full, etc., can be dangerous.	• Wear high-heeled shoes or ones which are loose and sloppy.
• Buy supportive underwear, such as support bras and maternity girdles, to help with extra weight.	• Neglect her appearance – looking and feeling a mess for nine months can be depressing.
• Choose lightweight, soft layers of clothing for winter warmth, or fine, airy fabrics for summer.	
• Choose comfortable footwear – feet may swell.	

Rest and exercise

DO	DON'T
• Get plenty of sleep – eight hours a night and a midday rest if possible.	• Worry about insomnia, as it is common during pregnancy.
• Make sure the bed and bedding are comfortable.	• Eat a large or indigestible meal before going to bed.
• Check the room is well ventilated.	• Give up all physical exercise because she thinks she must rest all the time.
• Practise relaxation exercises if sleeping is difficult.	• Put too much strain on her back with lifting heavy objects or stretching.
• Check with her doctor about continuing with strenuous sports.	• Continue with exercise if it is painful.
• Do plenty of walking, some gentle swimming or cycling.	
• Enrol in an exercise class for pregnant women.	

Posture

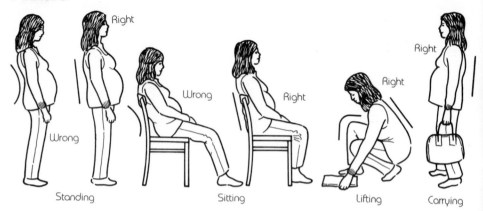

Standing   Sitting   Lifting   Carrying

Emotions

During pregnancy hormonal secretions have an influence upon the emotions of the pregnant woman. She will be prone to:

- Extreme reactions to unimportant things.
- Swings of mood, from the heights of pleasure and excitement to the depths of despair and unhappiness.
- Bouts of crying, anxiety, depression and confusion.

She can be helped by:

- Her own understanding that this is normal; taking care of her appearance; getting to know the facts about pregnancy, birth and child rearing; involving herself with other people and outside activities.
- Her partner, who can give her: constant reassurance, loving care and understanding; active help with household tasks; involvement in social activities; help with preparation for the baby's arrival; supervision and help with her fitness programme.
- Friends and relations who can give sensible help with other children or household tasks; offer encouragement; arrange social occasions.
- Her medical team of doctor, midwife, social worker, etc., with specific medical matters.

Father's role

The partner of the pregnant woman can easily feel left out. He can be encouraged to take an active part during pregnancy by:

- involving him in the preparations for the baby's arrival – buying clothing and equipment, preparing a room, etc. • showing him how vital his help with household tasks is • explaining how he can help with his partner's emotional needs and giving him opportunities to express his own fears or doubts • encouraging him to attend classes in parenthood and preparation for birth, so that he can help his partner before, during and after the birth • making him feel that a father is just as important to a child as a mother and giving him the confidence to tackle the job.

Physical changes

The output of hormones during pregnancy ensures that vital organs and functions will support the developing foetus. This means that:

- the volume of blood increases • the heart enlarges to enable it to work harder • the lungs work harder and there may be periods of breathlessness • the kidneys clean 50 per cent more blood and the bladder gets rid of more urine • the ligaments and the joints become softer and more flexible.

Also ● the skin may become more pigmented, stretch marks may appear and the skin may become dry or oily ● hair may become greasy, or dry and brittle ● nails may split or break ● gums and teeth may be more prone to infection.

These changes mean that a woman must be extra careful with diet, hygiene and dental care during pregnancy. Weight gain, for example, should be no more than 11–12 kg (24–6 lb) – see chart on page 29.

Minor ailments of pregnancy such as constipation, tiredness, heartburn, backache, etc., can usually be cleared up with a change of diet, intake of more fluids, more rest, etc.

The basic rules are:
● Never take unprescribed medication.
● Consult a chemist for minor complaints, the clinic nurse or doctor if a condition gets worse.
● Try simple remedies first.
● Some conditions, such as pregnancy sickness, will pass in time.
● Giving up smoking and/or alcohol will always improve health.
● A positive attitude to health is beneficial.

Medical care

The team of medical people involved includes: the general practitioner (GP); community midwife; consultant obstetrician; district nurse; health visitor; social worker; nursing ancillary (not qualified).

The pregnant woman can receive antenatal care at:
● her GP's clinic ● the community antenatal clinic ● the hospital antenatal unit.

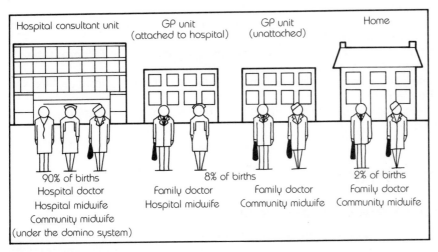

Hospital consultant unit	GP unit (attached to hospital)	GP unit (unattached)	Home
90% of births Hospital doctor Hospital midwife Community midwife (under the domino system)	8% of births Family doctor Hospital midwife	Family doctor Community midwife	2% of births Family doctor Community midwife

Who delivers where

The antenatal clinic will provide:
● Routine checks at the first visit (personal details and medical history will be noted); a cooperation card for filling in at every visit; an opportunity to discuss the pregnancy.
● Regular monitoring of the mother and the foetus.
● Special tests when necessary.
● Free iron and vitamin tablets.
● Advice on diet, infant feeding, relaxation techniques, exercises and parenthood classes.
● Opportunities to meet and talk with other pregnant women.

Tests during pregnancy

Routine tests	Special tests
Urine tests – to check for kidney infections	Ultra-sound scan – to check estimated date of delivery (EDD), multiple pregnancies, physical abnormalities, etc.
Height and shoe size – to check size of pelvic outlet	Alpha foetoprotein (AFP) – to check for spina bifida, multiple pregnancies, etc.
Weight – to check growth of foetus	Foetoscopy – to check for brain abnormalities, blood disorders, physical defects
Internal or external abdominal examinations – to confirm the pregnancy and size of uterus	Amniocentesis – to detect defects such as spina bifida, Down's syndrome
Cervical smear test – may be given to check for cancer or abnormalities	Chorionic villi test – to diagnose chromosomal abnormalities is undergoing trials. It can be carried out at 8–40 weeks and could replace amniocentesis
Blood pressure – to check for abnormalities such as pre-eclampsia (see below)	
Blood test – to find blood group and haemoglobin level, detect virus infections	
Foetal heartbeat – to confirm that the foetus is still alive	
Fingers, feet, ankles – to check for swelling	

The majority of pregnancies are straightforward, but sometimes things can go wrong.

For example:

- Miscarriage – the accidental ending of a pregnancy, known as a natural abortion up to the 28th week.
- Ectopic pregnancy – fertilised egg begins to develop in the Fallopian tube instead of the womb.
- Ante-partum haemorrhage – vaginal bleeding which can indicate problems with the placenta.
- Pre-eclampsia (toxaemia) – high blood pressure which can cause premature labour.

Preparations

Getting baby's room ready

Thoroughly clean the room. Make sure it is not damp or draughty. Decorate it attractively and have a warm floor covering and thick curtains. Put safety catches on the windows, provide a safe, efficient form of heating and have some fittings for subdued light. A comfortable chair and plenty of storage space will also be useful.

Buying equipment and clothing

Important points when choosing are:

- safety
- hygiene
- good design
- cost
- durability
- quality
- size
- aesthetics
- child appeal.

It is important just to buy essential clothing and equipment before the birth;

- some equipment may be borrowed or obtained secondhand
- try factory

shops and market stalls for keen prices be handmade, but remember safety are usually available or credit cards may be used.

- some clothing and equipment can
- look for the BSI label
- credit terms

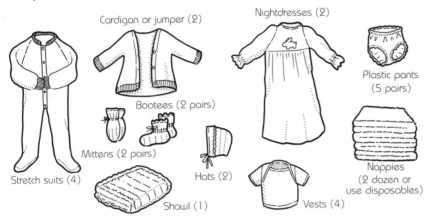

Cardigan or jumper (2)

Nightdresses (2)

Plastic pants (5 pairs)

Bootees (2 pairs)

Mittens (2 pairs)

Hats (2)

Stretch suits (4)

Shawl (1)

Vests (4)

Nappies (2 dozen or use disposables)

The new baby's clothing (layette)

Pre-birth planning

A few weeks before the birth:

- Arrange for any other children to be cared for during the confinement.
- See if the father can get paternity leave.
- Arrange for transport to hospital or collect the items needed for a home birth.
- Make a list of useful phone numbers – taxi, doctor, maternity unit, partner's place of work, etc.
- Have a case ready containing necessities for the hospital confinement.

The pregnant woman can discuss with her GP or midwife:

- How she will feed her baby.
- A 'birth plan', that is, how she wishes to give birth.
- Analgesics (pain-killers).
- Bonding immediately after birth.
- Her partner's involvement at the birth.

Pupil participation

Working briefs

Antenatal care

1. Perinatal mortality

Group work (Triggers)

Perinatal mortality in England and Wales by mother's country of birth 1984 (selected)

Mother's country of birth	Rate per thousand
All	10.1
United Kingdom	9.7
Australia, Canada, New Zealand	6.0
India	13.6
Bangladesh	14.1
West Indies	13.4
Pakistan	16.9

Mortality statistics: perinatal and infant, 1984 (OPCS)

Referring to the table on page 33, discuss in groups the possible reasons why a pregnant woman's country of birth can be related to the healthy birth of her child.

2. High risk categories during pregnancy

Group work (Triggers)

Make a series of cards like the ones given here as examples. Use them as 'triggers' to discuss why some situations or conditions present a threat to pregnancy. Allow each person in the group to speak for two minutes about one of the triggers.

Sample cards

3. Weight gain

Class work (Fact file)

Weight booklet

Produce a booklet suitable for pregnant women which will give information about:

- Minimum and maximum permissible weight gain during pregnancy. Use the weight gain chart on page 29. Remember that a reasonable weight gain of 11–12 kg (24–6 lb) is acceptable and necessary.
- The dangers of being overweight; for example, the increased chances of needing a Caesarean section and of putting strain on the heart.
- Suggestions for keeping weight gain at acceptable levels.
- The foods and drinks to avoid and those which will be beneficial.

Test the value of your booklet by giving copies to pregnant friends or relations. Was it well received? Did they find the advice helpful? How could your booklet be improved?

4. Diet

Problem-solving assignments

Assignment A Vida leaves home early in the morning for work. She is suffering quite badly from early morning pregnancy sickness.

a) Give some suggestions for her early morning breakfasts.
b) Plan and make some nutritious snacks she could take to work to eat later in the morning when feelings of nausea have passed.

(See example on page 55.)

Assignment B Betty and Dave have two small children and are expecting a third. They have a low income. Plan one day's meals for them. The meals must be nutritious, varied, interesting and economical.

Make one of the main-meal dishes.

Assignment C Make a chart which is easy to understand and illustrates some of the dishes that would be a good choice during pregnancy. Show the nutrients each dish contains and highlight those which are especially important during pregnancy.

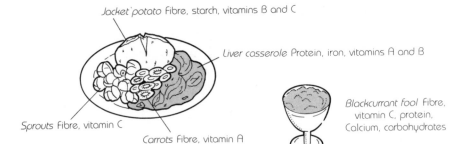

Jacket potato Fibre, starch, vitamins B and C

Liver casserole Protein, iron, vitamins A and B

Blackcurrant fool Fibre, vitamin C, protein, Calcium, carbohydrates

Sprouts Fibre, vitamin C

Carrots Fibre, vitamin A

Sample meal

5. Clothing

Individual work (Survey)

Study the maternity fashions in the following illustration – you can see similar ones in shops and mail-order catalogues. Make a reasoned assessment of each one, commenting on these points:

- Are they well designed?
- Is the fabric suitable?
- Could they be adapted for use after pregnancy?
- Colour schemes?
- Are they 'easy care'?
- Are they fashionable and comfortable to wear?
- Are the local maternity fashion prices good value for money?

Carry out the same exercise for:

a) underclothes   b) outerwear   c) footwear.

Which shops do you think sell the best maternity wear at reasonable prices?

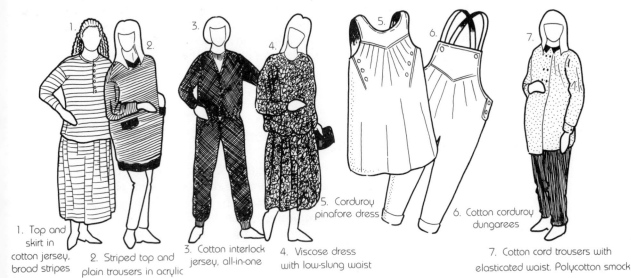

1. Top and skirt in cotton jersey, broad stripes

2. Striped top and plain trousers in acrylic

3. Cotton interlock jersey, all-in-one

4. Viscose dress with low-slung waist

5. Corduroy pinafore dress

6. Cotton corduroy dungarees

7. Cotton cord trousers with elasticated waist. Polycotton smock

Maternity fashions

6. The father's role

Individual work (Poster)

The role of the expectant father is very important during pregnancy. To encourage him to play an active part, design a display poster which could go on a wall in the antenatal clinic or the doctor's surgery. You could use a humorous approach with cartoon figures, but the message you must convey is a serious one.

7. The antenatal clinic   Individual or class work (Visit)

Try to visit an antenatal clinic in your area. It could be one which is attached to a GP's surgery, a hospital or a community clinic. The clinic doctor, midwife, nurse or health visitor may be able to show you round and answer some of your questions. Be prepared to listen carefully and ask sensible questions. Do a follow-up report using the following format:

- *General information* – date and time of visit, name and address of clinic, names of the people you met and the person who showed you round.
- Describe the layout of the clinic and the plan of each room.
- Note the atmosphere of the clinic – was it busy, efficient, cheerful, etc?
- List the staff who run the clinic and their duties.
- What is the purpose of the clinic and what kinds of tests and treatments are carried out?
- Find out and report on what happens the first time a pregnant woman visits, the follow-up procedures and frequency of visits.
- List the advantages of regular attendance at the clinic and any disadvantages there may be.
- Could you suggest any improvements?

Complete a report as suggested.

Preparations to be made

8. The baby's room   Individual work (Problem-solving)

Errol and Belinda live in a small terraced house. They want to make the back bedroom into a nursery, but it faces north and is therefore rather dark and cold.

a) Suggest ways in which they could make the room look cheerful and bright.
b) Advise them on methods of heating which are safe and economical. Suggest floor covering and curtains which will give added warmth.
c) The ceiling is high so they want to put a frieze round the walls to break up the depth. Design a frieze which is attractive, colourful and stimulating.

(See example on page 56.)

9. The baby's equipment   Group work (Trails)

Divide into groups of two or three. Each group should select one or more pieces of baby equipment to study and then compare different designs and makes. Study equipment such as prams, pushchairs, cots, baby baths, high chairs, potties, baby alarms, feeding equipment, room heaters, safety lights, baby carriers and slings, toiletries and baby baskets. If possible bring some items with you to discuss. After you have done your research, set up a display of articles, pictures, magazine reports and your findings. The class can then move from display to display asking questions of the group who set it up.

(See example on page 56.)

10. Consumer information   Class work (Market research)

Compare and evaluate the various methods of purchasing expensive baby equipment. Copy the chart opposite into your book, complete the ticks in each column. Give your assessment for each method by using these symbols:

| | ☺ Very good method | ☺ Satisfactory method | ☹ Unsatisfactory in many ways |

Payment by :	Advantages				Disadvantages				Assessment
	Spreads out payments	Easy method to use	No deposit needed	No interest charged	High interest rate	Article may be repossessed	Easy to take on too much debt	A long-term system	
Cash		✓	✓						
Credit Card (Access, etc.)									
Store Credit Card (Mothercare, etc.)									
Hire Purchase									
Extended Terms									
Mail Order	✓								
Bank Loan					✓				

11. Baby's clothing

Individual work (Investigation)

Trace and copy these outlines of baby clothes into your book or make a special file. For each garment:

● Put in design features, such as ribbing, decorations, seams, method of fastening, fabric pattern.
● Explain the type of fabric they could be made from and give reasons.
● Suggest colour schemes, appliqué, embroidery, etc.
● State the fabric finishes which could be applied to make the garments easier to launder, safer to wear, etc.
● Give laundering instructions for each one.
● Show the importance of any safety features.

(See example on page 57.)

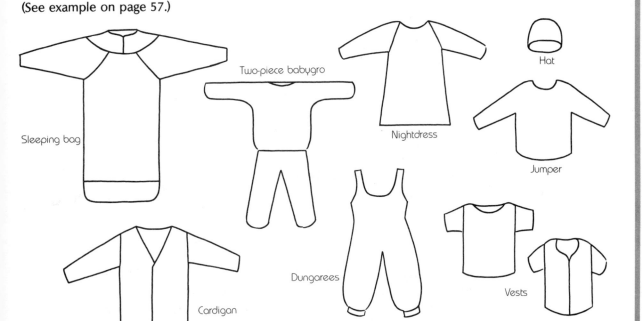

Sleeping bag
Two-piece babygro
Nightdress
Hat
Jumper
Cardigan
Dungarees
Vests

12. Clothing and equipment   Class work (Brainstorming)

Few young couples who are just starting a family are able to go out and buy everything they would like for the expected baby. Discuss suggestions for obtaining clothing or equipment as cheaply as possible; for example, from jumble sales.

13. Planning for the birth   Class work (Debate)

'Expectant fathers should be encouraged to be at the birth of their child.' Divide into two groups to discuss this issue, one group for it and one group against. Elect a spokesperson to put forward the arguments for each side and then take a vote to decide on whether the motion is carried or not.

Written work

Fact finding exercises

Explain the following terms:

paternity leave   cooperation card   domino system
obstetric history   insomnia   relaxation exercises
natural abortion   pre-eclampsia   birth plan

What are the possible effects of:

high amounts of caffeine in the diet?
having a small pelvic area?
taking unprescribed drugs during pregnancy?
placing the cot under the window of the nursery?
using cheap and/or highly scented soaps and other toiletries for a baby?

What is the difference between:

infant mortality rate	and	perinatal mortality rate?
natural fibres	and	synthetic fibres?
antenatal care	and	postnatal care?
an obstetrician	and	a GP?

Give reasons why:

Highly spiced and greasy foods are not a good choice during pregnancy.
High-heeled shoes should not be worn during pregnancy.
The knees should be bent when lifting heavy objects.
The pregnant woman may have bouts of depression.
The pregnant woman must give special care to her teeth, hair and skin during pregnancy.
A cervical smear test is part of the antenatal care routine.

Application of knowledge

1. Describe the work of three members of the medical team who care for the pregnant woman.

2. Describe the following three special tests given during pregnancy. State at what stage during pregnancy they are given, and their purpose:
   a) ultra-sound scan   b) amniocentesis   c) AFP screening.

3. Write a paragraph about each of the following difficulties which may occur in the late stages of pregnancy and suggest ways of relieving them:
   a) tiredness   b) backache   c) varicose veins   c) sleeplessness.

Data response

Nappy costs and care

Terry nappies – cost per month	£	All-in-one-disposables – cost per month	
Purchase cost for two dozen, worked out over $2\frac{1}{2}$-year period – cost per month	= 1.53	6 per day at an average cost of 10.3 pence each 180 per month	= £18.54
Disposable nappy liners, 183 per month	= 2.20		
Sterilising solution, 5p per day – per month	= 1.55		
Waterproof pants 1 pair per month	= 0.55		
Washing costs per month	= 4.38		
Fabric conditioner per month	= 0.65		
Tumble drying per month	= 0.72		
Total cost per month	£11.58	Total cost per month	£18.54

Nappy Advisory Service

	Marks
1. How much could you save per month by using Terry nappies rather than disposables?	1
2. How much extra could you save if you did not use fabric conditioner?	1
3. It is better to dry Terry nappies outdoors when possible. If you only use the tumble dryer for six months of the year, how much would you save?	1
4. Suggest four circumstances when the use of disposable nappies would be an advantage.	4
5. Describe the treatment given to the used nappy from the time it is removed from the baby to the time it is put away clean.	6
6. Discuss the causes and treatment of nappy rash.	3 + 4
	20

Free response

'Evidence suggests that persuading mothers not to smoke cigarettes would do more to reduce infant mortality in the UK than any other single action.'

DHSS, in *Prevention and Health*, 1977

Comment upon this statement. Explain the effects of cigarette smoking upon the developing foetus and suggest ways in which the pregnant woman can be encouraged to give it up.

Self-assessment

Photocopy and complete the self-assessment chart on page 161, inserting the following topics under 'The work I have done includes':

Antenatal care:
1. Reasons for care
2. Diet during pregnancy
3. Clothing during pregnancy
4. Rest and exercise
5. Posture
6. Emotions
7. Father's role
8. Physical changes
9. Minor ailments
10. Medical care
11. The antenatal clinic
12. Routine and special tests
13. Problems in pregnancy

Preparations:
1. The baby's room
2. Buying equipment
3. Baby clothing
4. A few weeks before birth.

Photocopy and complete the self-marking plan on page 162 for the thirteen working briefs in this unit.

Birth and Postnatal Care

Core Information

Labour and birth

The onset of labour

A few weeks before birth the baby's head will pass into the cavity of the pelvis, that is, it will 'engage'.

When the pregnancy has reached 'full term', at 40 weeks, hormones will trigger the birth. Pre-term babies are those born a few weeks before term; post-mature babies are those born a few weeks after term. The following illustration shows the positions for birth.

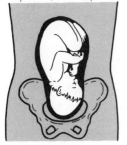
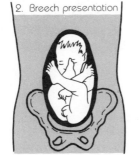

1. Cephalic (normal) position   2. Breech presentation   3. Transverse presentation

Positions for birth

1. The cephalic (normal) position for birth – head first

2. Breech presentation – bottom or feet first

3. Transverse presentation – lying across the womb.

Positions 2 and 3 may need a Caesarean section.

The onset of labour is usually spontaneous and signalled by a 'show'; that is, the small blood-stained mucus plug is dislodged from the cervix. The 'waters break', which means that the membranes rupture and there is a gush of liquid – the amniotic fluid. Contractions or labour pains occur every few minutes and become increasingly severe.

Any or all of these signs indicate that the birth is imminent and the pregnant woman should:

● ring the hospital   ● contact her partner   ● collect outdoor clothing and ready-packed case   ● ring for an ambulance or other form of transport   ● for a home confinement, ring the midwife, check the room is ready and have a bath.

A first labour will last on average for 12–14 hours, whereas subsequent labours will last on average for 7 hours.

When she is admitted to the maternity unit, the pregnant woman will see the midwife, who will consult the woman's notes and check:

- whether her waters have broken
- the baby's position
- the foetal heartbeat
- how frequent the contractions are
- the woman's blood pressure, pulse and temperature
- how far the cervix is dilated (open).

Birth

There are three stages of labour:

Stage 1 starts with regular contractions of the uterus which cause the cervix to open, or 'dilate'.

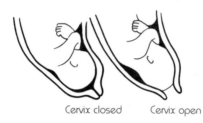

Cervix closed   Cervix open

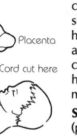

Cord tied off here and here

Placenta

Cord cut here

Cutting the cord

When fully dilated the cervix is approximately 10 cm (4 in) in diameter. The baby's head begins to move further into the pelvis. This stage can take several hours and there is then a transitional stage of up to an hour until the start of Stage 2.

Stage 2 The bag of waters will burst if it has not already done so. There are bearing down contractions to allow the baby to be pushed slowly and smoothly down the birth canal. The head is born first, followed by the shoulders and the trunk. The umbilical cord is tied and cut. This stage lasts between one and two hours for a first baby, between 15 and 20 minutes for subsequent babies.

Stage 3 completes the process. The afterbirth (placenta) is expelled. The uterus continues gradually contracting and shrinking back to its original size.

Care during labour

Medical care

Stage 1 Foetal heartbeat constantly monitored. Cervical dilation checked periodically. Anaesthetist will visit to discuss pain relief. The progress of labour may be charted on a partogram. Blood pressure, urine and temperature tests are given.

Stage 2 Analgesics may be administered. The midwife will advise when to push, when to relax, breathe deeply or pant. She will encourage the baby's head downwards and ease out the head and body carefully. An episiotomy will be given if needed. The midwife will wipe the baby's eyes, nose and mouth and remove fluid from the nose and upper air passages. The cord will be tied and cut.

Stage 3 When the placenta is delivered it will be checked to see that it is complete. Mother and baby will be cleaned and the mother will be stitched if necessary.

Care from the partner

Persuade woman to relax, be generally supportive, keep calm and provide companionship. Make sure the medical staff are aware of the type of birth preferred, for example, natural childbirth. Give reassurance.

Give sips of water to the woman, mop brow, sponge down with cold water. Encourage woman with pushing, help with breathing and relaxation techniques. Hold mother and baby close when birth is over, giving bodily warmth.

Time for bonding between parents and baby.

Pain relief

Women feel different levels of pain during labour. Some find that understanding what is happening and the use of breathing and relaxation techniques give them sufficient pain relief. Other methods include:

- Inhalation – breathing in a 50:50 mixture of nitrous oxide and oxygen through a face mask controlled by the woman.
- Epidural injection into the back during the first and second stages of labour.
- Pethidine – a pain-relieving drug given as an injection during the first stage.
- Hypnosis and acupuncture.

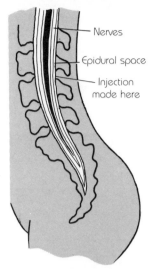

Epidural anaesthetic

Complications during labour

Induction If labour is delayed or there is a medical reason for bringing it forward, it can be induced artificially. This can be done by:

- Rupturing the membranes.
- Giving oxytocin (a hormone) as a drip into a vein.
- Administering prostaglandin pessaries, a gel containing a mixture of hormones.

Reasons for induction include:
- baby is well over term • risk to mother's health • complications expected • foetal distress symptoms • social reasons.

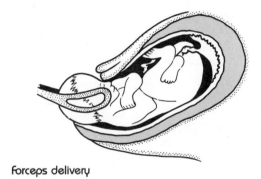

Forceps delivery

Forceps delivery Carried out by a doctor if the woman is becoming exhausted or the baby is showing signs of distress.

Episiotomy A small cut made in the perineum to make the delivery of the baby easier. It may be necessary if:

- The baby's head is large.
- The perineum will not stretch sufficiently and is in danger of tearing.
- The delivery is breech or forceps.

The cut is stitched up under local anaesthetic after the birth.

Ventouse (suction) delivery A special cap attached to a suction pump is attached to the head of the baby. The doctor pulls on this to help the baby emerge.

Electronic foetal monitoring (EFM) A method of recording the baby's heartbeat and the progress of labour. Usually used in high-risk pregnancies.

Malpresentation Usually a breech presentation. Forceps, an epidural or a Caesarean section may be necessary.

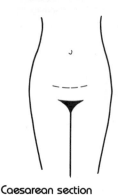

Caesarean section

Caesarean section This is an operation to remove the baby from the uterus by cutting through the abdominal wall and the uterus, through a bikini-line incision (see diagram). About six births in every hundred take place by this operation. It may be preplanned or an emergency and may be necessary if:

- the baby is too big to be delivered normally
- it is a multiple birth
- it is a breech birth
- there are complications with the mother's health
- the baby is distressed.

A **premature** (pre-term) baby is born before 36 weeks.
A **low birthweight** baby is born weighing under 2.5 kg ($5\frac{1}{2}$ lb)
A pre-term baby of only 24 weeks will sometimes survive. Multiple births may cause complications.

All these types of baby need special care during and after birth. They may need foetal monitoring and delivery by Caesarean section. After birth they may need to spend some time in an incubator in a special care unit.

Postnatal care and tests

Mother

Stitches will be removed a few days after birth.
The perineum will heal quite quickly and the breasts will produce milk. The uterus will shrink, especially if the mother is breast feeding. All body functions will return to normal.
Postnatal exercises and a careful check on weight are encouraged.

1. Tighten seat muscles, pull tummy in and feel spine press down on bed.
2. Tighten muscles round birth canal, as though stopping yourself passing water.

3. Turn body here from side to side slowly, leave legs and feet in place.

Easy-to-practise exercise for after the birth

Normally, new mothers will feel elated after the birth, but a few days later may experience **postnatal depression** (PND) due to fluctuating hormone levels. This usually passes quite quickly, but occasionally develops into a severe form of PND which needs medical treatment.
The mother should have a postnatal checkup about six weeks after delivery. This will:

Baby

Soon after birth an identification bracelet will be placed on the baby, who will be weighed and measured and have the diameter of the skull measured. The baby will be examined to check that hips, heart, lungs, abdomen, inside mouth and bowel movements are all normal.

Automatic reflexes checked are:
1. rooting 2. grasping 3. sucking
4. stepping 5. placing 6. startle
7. moro.

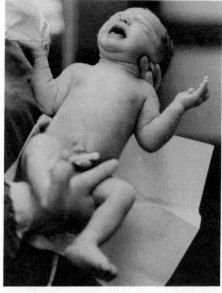

A newborn baby

The new baby will usually cry and needs sleep, cuddling, cleaning, warmth and food.

- Check the mother's weight, blood pressure and urine.
- Check the mother's emotional condition.
- Check that everything is healing well.
- Give contraceptive advice if required.
- Involve a routine smear test.
- Be an opportunity to discuss any problems.

The baby may:
- be covered in vernix
- be covered in fine hair ● have eyes that are sticky and blood-shot
- have birthmarks ● have a misshapen head ● have a rash
- develop jaundice and look yellow.

A full-term baby will usually:
- look rounded and plump
- be a good colour ● weigh 2.7–3.6 kg (6–8 lb) ● be 50–2 cm (20–1 in) long ● measure 33–5 cm (13–14 in) round the skull.

Caring for the newborn baby

Bonding

It is important that as soon as possible after birth close emotional feelings (bonding) develop between mother and baby, and between father and baby. This can be encouraged by:
- cuddling ● sharing body warmth ● breast feeding ● eye contact
- touching and caressing ● soothing voice contact.

Feeding

Breast feeding is usually considered the best option because:
- it provides nutritionally balanced food ● it is clean ● breast milk is easily digested ● milk is at the correct temperature ● breast milk contains the mother's antibodies ● it strengthens natural bonding.

Possible difficulties are:
- baby being unable to suck properly ● sore or inverted nipples
- inadequate flow of milk ● mother being uncomfortable, embarrassed or anxious ● inability to check how much milk the baby is taking ● social reasons.

These problems can usually be solved with the help of a midwife, health visitor, baby clinic or organisation such as the National Childbirth Trust or the La Leche League.

Breast feeding should start immediately after birth. Many mothers use the 'on demand' system and the baby quite quickly gets into a three- to four-hour feeding routine.

Bottle feeding is more complex, more expensive and more likely to cause gastro-infections, and is time-consuming to prepare. But it may be essential if:
- the mother is unwell ● she goes out to work ● the baby is getting insufficient breast milk or not thriving.

Breast feeding can be supplemented with bottle feeds if necessary. It is essential that for bottle feeding:
- all the equipment is sterilised and the feed is made up hygienically ● the correct proportions of milk powder and water are used ● boiling water is used
- only specialised infant milk powders are used ● the baby is given a milk formula that suits him or her ● any unused made-up milk is thrown away
- out-of-date milk powder is not used.

Returning home

The usual stay in hospital is five to six days but some mothers only have a 24-hour or 48-hour stay. After a medical checkup they are allowed home into the care of the midwife or health visitor for between ten and fourteen days. The hospital stay can last longer if there are any complicating circumstances.

The new mother will need:

● plenty of sleep and rest   ● a good diet with lots of fluids   ● fresh air and reasonable exercise   ● love and support from her partner, family and friends.

The new baby will need:

● warmth – a fairly constant temperature of 20–1 °C (68–70 °F) and warm clothing and bedding in winter   ● food – a satisfactory milk diet until about 4 months old   ● sleep – the baby will sleep for about 60 per cent of the day
● protection – from infection and disease and from accidents   ● love and security – from the parents, siblings and relations   ● hygiene – bathing and general cleaning throughout the day.

Undress baby and wrap in a towel. Clean face and hair

Soap the body, holding baby on lap

Rinse baby in the bath. Dry well, apply talcum powder. Put on clean clothes

Bath-time routine

Nappies must be thoroughly washed and sterilised, or they will cause nappy rash.

Crying

This is the only way that a baby can show distress. A baby may cry because he or she:

● is hungry   ● is too cold or too hot   ● is in pain because of colic, uncomfortable clothing, etc.   ● has a dirty nappy   ● is overtired   ● is frightened by a sudden noise, jerky movement, bright light, etc.   ● is lonely and wants picking up.

Many of these problems are easily solved. Persistent crying should not be ignored and help can be obtained from the GP, health visitor or baby clinic.

The new parents should soon develop a daily **routine** which will include:

● baby's routine care   ● time for other children   ● sleep, rest, fresh air and exercise   ● household chores   ● food buying and family mealtimes
● recreational activities   ● time for themselves.

Contraception

Menstruation will start again five to eight weeks after the birth. Sexual relationships can be resumed a few weeks after the birth, when both parents feel ready. A woman **can** become pregnant again during the first few months after a birth, **and** while she is breast feeding. Contraceptive advice will be offered at the postnatal examination or from:

● health visitor   ● family planning clinic   ● chemist   ● books and magazines.

Advice is free. Some contraceptives are free on prescription and some FP clinics have special youth information sessions.

Pupil participation

Working briefs

1. Birth   Varied group work

Divide into three groups. Each group can study one of the assignments below. After a discussion, carry out the suggested work. When finished, get together as a class, explain the work you have done and ask for comments.

Assignment A Jenny has strong views about the type of birth she wants. She wants it to be as natural as possible. She therefore decides to write a letter to her maternity unit setting out her wishes as clearly and politely as possible. These are some of her requests:

● the birth is not to be induced unless for urgent medical reasons   ● a routine episiotomy is not to be given   ● no mechanical intervention or drugs are to be used unless in an emergency   ● the father is to be present throughout   ● the baby is to be given to the mother immediately after the birth.

Add other requests to this list and draft a suitably polite letter for Jenny to send or hand in to the maternity unit.

Assignment B Jane is keen to try the 'domino' system of birth, which is available in her area. She has had one uncomplicated confinement and she wants to remain under the care of her own GP and midwife, and return home as soon as possible after the birth.

Draw up a list of informative points about this method, which will help her to decide whether or not to try it, and also help her to plan the birth.

Assignment C Donna is having her first baby and is keen to have the birth at home. Her home conditions are suitable, but her doctor would prefer her to have a hospital confinement and feels unable to provide medical care for a home delivery.

Draft out a letter from Donna to her district health authority requesting maternity cover by a local midwife for a home confinement.

2. Medical terms   Individual work (fact file)

There are a lot of scientific and medical terms connected with pregnancy and birth which you will need to remember. As a quick reference, make a dictionary of the most important words and terms, giving a brief description or meaning. A selection is given below:

Abortion – loss of the foetus, spontaneous or induced
Breech presentation – baby in uterus with feet or bottom towards cervix

Colostrum – the first milk secreted by the breasts
Dilation – the widening of the cervix during delivery
Epidural – a spinal anaesthetic sometimes used during labour
Forceps – metal instrument used to aid delivery of the foetus
Gynaecologist – a doctor who specialises in women's medical conditions.

3. Case histories   Class discussion (Problem-solving)

Read the situations which are given below. In the follow-up class discussion be prepared to put forward ideas to help with Jeff, Sue, Darshini and Rajir's problems.

Case history A. Jeff is proud of the fact that he is going to be a new dad. He has helped his wife with household jobs and has given lots of support during pregnancy. He knows she wants him to be there when the baby is born and he longs to see his baby the minute it arrives, but he is beginning to feel worried about it. His friend at work told him that when he attended his wife's confinement he felt useless and in the way and nearly passed out.

What advice would you give to Jeff? Where could he go for professional advice?

Case history B. Sue has had a trouble-free pregnancy and has kept cheerful and happy. As the time for the birth approaches she begins to worry about how she will cope with a painful delivery. She feels she is a real coward at times and is frightened of making a fool of herself.

Who can reassure Sue and give her truthful and practical advice about pain control during childbirth? What might such a person suggest?

Case history C. Darshini and Rajir both have good, well-paid jobs and they have a small, comfortable house. Darshini would like to return to work as soon as possible after the birth of her baby, but Rajir thinks she ought to remain at home with the baby for at least twelve months. This problem is causing friction between them, especially as Darshini knows that without her salary their standard of living will be a lot lower and that if she is away from her job for over a year her chances of promotion will be much reduced.

Make a list of the advantages of Darshini's being with her baby at home for a year, and also suggest some alternatives, or ways of compromising.

4. New baby   Individual work (Investigation)

Begin to create a set of **profiles** of babies and children at various ages and stages of development.
Your first one will be of the new baby.
Your second one will be at six months old, then one year, two, three, four, five and six years.
You will then have a complete developmental record of the young child. Try to include:

● brief written descriptions   ● developmental progress   ● milestones
● drawings and/or photographs.

Your work should be based on an 'average' child.

(See example on page 57.)

5. Postnatal depression

Class work (Rounds)

Because of fluctuating hormone levels, the new mother usually suffers from a period of PND. Think of ways in which she can be helped and then go round the group, each person finishing the sentence:
PND can be helped by a new mother's partner if he . . .
or PND can be helped by a new mother's doctor or midwife if they . . .
or PND can be helped by a new mother's friends and relations if they . . .

6. Postnatal care

Class work (Brainstorming)

Everyone in the group should think of what he or she considers to be some important aspects of postnatal dos and don'ts. Then go quickly round the group to get everyone's suggestions.
Examples:

DO	have a sensible diet	DON'T	try to spring clean!
	take plenty of rest		worry about unimportant
	have the special medical		things
	checks.		listen to well-meant advice
			from people who are not
			well informed.

Follow this up by discussing and deciding which are the important issues. Record the results of your discussions in the form of a table.

7. The new baby

Individual work (Investigation)

These are examples of letters received by parentcare magazines. What replies would you give?

My milk has become rather thin and watery-looking since I returned from hospital. Will it still be strong enough for my baby?

My new baby has a long crying spell every evening from about six o'clock and seems to be in pain. My neighbour says it could be colic. What does she mean and what can I do about it?

My baby is four weeks old and she often appears to have a squint in one or both eyes. Do you think this is permanent and will she need treatment?

My young baby has a rash of tiny white spots on and around his nose. What should I do about it?

8. Feeding
Individual work (Collaborative learning game)

The pictures below, which show how to make up a milk feed in a feeding bottle, are in the wrong sequence. State which is the correct order and do a similar guide for making up a feed using a measuring jug.

If you have the necessary equipment in your classroom, demonstrate how you would make up a milk feed for a four-week-old baby.

(See example on page 59.)

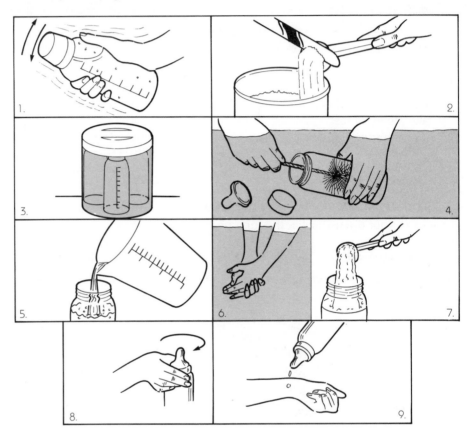

9. Nappy care
Individual work (Survey)

Make a five (or more) point plan for avoiding nappy rash and
a five (or more) point plan for dealing with nappy rash.

Example:

Avoiding nappy rash
- Never allow a baby to wear a dirty nappy for long periods.
- Use good quality baby toiletries.

Dealing with nappy rash
- Sterilise all nappies after use.
- Dry nappies out of doors whenever possible.

Do a snap survey amongst any mothers of young babies whom you know and ask them:

Has your baby ever had nappy rash? If so, what do you think was the cause? How did you deal with it? What methods would you recommend for dealing with it?

Collate your findings.

Written work

Fact finding exercises

1. Find out about and then write a paragraph on each of the following:
   Natural childbirth.
   The use of hypnosis or acupuncture during childbirth.
   The customs and preferences of some ethnic minority families during pregnancy and childbirth.
   The care of premature babies.
   Keeping feeding bottles and teats clean.

2. Write out a clear list of instructions for laundering nappies.

Application of knowledge

1. What is meant by:
   a forceps delivery   transverse presentation
   full term   the head being engaged
   a show   the waters breaking
   the cephalic position   a low birthweight baby?

2. Giving three reasons for each, explain why the following may be necessary:
   induction   Caesarean section   foetal monitoring.

3. Briefly explain the three stages of labour.

Short answer questions

1. What is the average length and average weight of a new born baby?

2. Name three nutrients found in cow's milk.

3. What is the difference between an episiotomy and an epidural?

4. How is pethidine administered?

5. Name three non-medical people who could give help and support to a woman during labour.

6. Why is an identification bracelet placed on a new baby in hospital?

7. Name and describe three automatic reflexes.

8. What is meant by 'vernix'?

Free response

1. Explain the importance of bonding and suggest ways in which it can be achieved between parent(s) and child in the immediate postnatal period.

2. Using the headings 'Rest', 'Diet', 'Exercise', 'Medical checks' and 'Emotional needs', describe the postnatal care of the new mother.

3. Plan a daily routine suitable for the mother of a new baby in the following family circumstances:
   a) Mother, first baby; father goes to work at 8.30 a.m., returns at 4.45 p.m.
   b) Mother, baby, one toddler; father at work all day.
   Begin your plan with the 6 a.m. feed and end at 10.30 p.m. Remember to include such things as household chores, meal preparation and shopping, rest periods and playing with any other children.

Data response

Perinatal mortality by social class, England and Wales 1984

Social class*	Rate per thousand live and still births
All	10.1
All legitimate	9.5
Of which:	
Professional	7.1
Intermediate	7.9
Skilled non-manual	8.2
Skilled manual	9.8
Semi-skilled	11.6
Unskilled	14.1

*Social class using father's occupation and employment status as recorded on the child's birth certificate.

Mortality statistics: perinatal and infant, 1984 (OPCS)

1. Explain the term 'perinatal mortality rate'.

2. Which social class has the highest rate per 1000?

3. Which social class has the lowest rate per 1000?

4. How is social class determined?

5. Suggest five reasons why the difference in the perinatal mortality rate is almost twice as high in the unskilled classes as in the professional class.

6. Describe some of the ways in which the government encourages good antenatal and postnatal care.

Self-assessment

Photocopy and complete the self-assessment chart on page 161, inserting the following topics under 'The work I have done includes':

Birth:
1. Stages of labour
2. Pain relief
3. Delivery
4. Complications
5. Partner's role

The new baby:
1. Profile
2. Feeding
3. Hygiene
4. Emotions

Postnatal care:
1. Medical
2. PND
3. Bonding.

Photocopy and complete the self-marking plan on page 162 for the nine working briefs in this unit.

Appendices – Study Area 1 ——————

Methods of recording and presenting results

Responsibilities for parenthood (page 9)

Example 1. Divorce (page 14)

Survey classmates, friends, adults, asking
'Is divorce too easy to obtain?'   YES/NO

The survey of the results can be recorded as a bar chart.

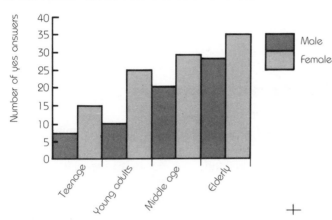

Number of people interviewed: 170

Example 2. Diet (page 15)

a) Prepare a detailed timetable of meal preparation throughout the day.
Leave a column to show the actual times.

Estimated time	Work plan	Actual time
11.30–11.35	Assemble ingredients and equipment	11.30–11.34
11.35–11.40	Cut up chicken and vegetables	11.34–11.40
12.00	Serve lunch	?

b) The protein value of your daily menus can be presented as a stick graph.

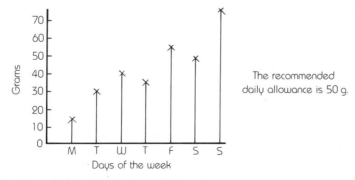

The recommended
daily allowance is 50 g.

Amounts of protein consumed during one week

Example 3.   Chromosomes (page 17)

Make up some sets of Identikit pictures. Assemble strips of various features which will slot in.

Show how your family characteristics pass from generation to generation.

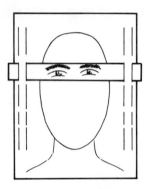
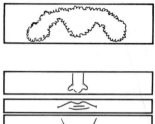

Curly blond hair

Bushy eyebrows
Narrow, blue eyes

Straight nose

Large mouth, thin lips

Pointed chin

Biological background (page 20)

Example 4.   Menstruation (page 25)

A simple book to be used to teach young and/or slow-learning children must:

● be easily understood   ● be colourful   ● be interesting   ● contain language that is easy to understand   ● not be too technical   ● contain clear diagrams.

Materials needed Strong card, pictures to cut out or copy from magazines, felt-tip pens, glue, plastic film or laminated card.

Planning

Book

or

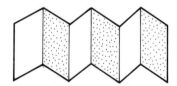

Size and *number* of pages?

Title? Examples – 'Growing up' or 'Just Like Mummy'.

Contents to include:

● what causes a period   ● how and when it starts   ● how to deal with it
● leading a normal life   ● dealing with minor discomforts.

Execution

Cover

Information pages

- When you are about 10 years old your body begins to change and develop.
- This is so that when you grow up you can have babies.
- Men produce sperm, women produce eggs. When the two join a baby is formed.
- A baby will grow inside a woman's tummy until it is big enough to be born.

Evaluation Check your planning – will the result be a teaching aid which will instruct a child sensitively and clearly about menstruation?
The wallchart or frieze given as a working brief for 'Foetal Development' can be planned and executed in the same way as your teaching booklet.

Example 5. Multiple pregnancies – A Survey (page 26)
This is an example of a pre-coded questionnaire which you could produce. Ask a responsible representative from each first-, second- and third-year class in your school to fill it in. The form teacher may help. You could also give the survey to a random sample of primary or junior school children.

QUESTIONNAIRE ABOUT TWINS, TRIPLETS AND QUADS

SCHOOL . . . . FORM . . . . . . NUMBER IN FORM . . . .

Y = yes, N = no

1. Are there any sets of twins in the form? **Y or N** ☐

2. Are the twins identical?
   I = Identical,
   NI = Non-identical **I or NI** ☐

3. Are they both: B = Boys,
   G = Girls, M = Mixed? **B or G or M** ☐

4. Racial grouping?
   WB = White British
   AB = Asian British
   WAB = West Indian/Afro British **WB or AB or WAB** ☐

5. Are there other sets of twins in the same family? **Y or N** ☐

6. Are there other sets of twins in their families?
   a) Mother's relatives. **Y or N** ☐
   b) Father's relatives. ☐

7. Are there any sets of triplets in the form? **Y or N** ☐

8. Are there any sets of quads in the form? (repeat the set of queries as for twins). **Y or N** ☐

You will have some statistical information which you can collate on bar and/or pie charts.

Finally, assess your results.

Pregnancy (page 28)

Example 6. Diet. A practical assignment (page 34)
Plan and make some nutritious mid-morning snacks suitable for a pregnant woman. Make up an individual serving of any of the following suggestions and put it in a lidded container ready for use.

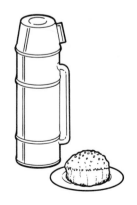

1. Oat-based crunchy cereal mixed with dried apricots, prunes, raisins, a few nuts, a spoonful of honey and some low-fat yoghurt.

2. A wholemeal pitta bread filled with mixed salad ingredients, flaked fish or hard boiled egg.

3. A flask of home made vegetable soup with a wholemeal roll.

4. Mixed bean salad (canned) mixed with diced cheese, chopped apple and tomato.

5. Home-baked muesli bar with a hot chocolate drink.

Write out the recipe you have used.

List the nutrients to be found in your snack, the cost and the time taken to make it.

Example 7.   The baby's room. A frieze (page 36)
Design a frieze which is attractive, colourful and stimulating.

Planning Discuss the possibilities.

- What type of theme will you use? Examples are animals, TV characters and numbers.
- Colour schemes – do you want bright, primary colours or muted pastels?
- Will it be drawn and then painted, or will the background be done and the figures then stuck on (either a painting or a collage)?
- Will it be flat, or textured with the use of fabrics, foil, string, fur or textured paper?
- How will you attach it to the wall?
- How wide and how long do you want it?
- Could it be a group project and then be presented to a children's home or a playgroup when finished?

Example 8.   Baby's equipment (page 36)

1. Anatomical potty – curves round baby's bottom, supports baby's back

2. Plastic potty with lid

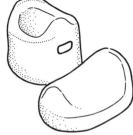

3. Potty chair, high back and sides. Removable inner bowl

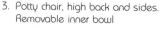

7. Musical toilet – music starts when baby sits down, seat removes for use on normal size toilet

4. Firm, wide-based, plastic potty

5. Inflatable potty – comes for travelling with disposable liners

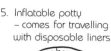

6. Fun potty – strong, stable, easy to clean

Select an item of baby equipment, for example the potty. Collect pictures of different types of potties and, if possible, actual models to set up a display. Try to find out the prices and consider how easy they would be to clean. The potty chair and musical toilet are expensive – are they worth the money? What disadvantages might the inflatable potty have? Give clear judgements on all the equipment chosen.

Example 9.   Item for a child (page 37)
If your examination syllabus requires you to make an item for a child's use, you could make one of the garments outlined on page 37. Remember, any nightwear for children must be made with flame-resistant fabric.

Planning

- Consider the task you are going to set yourself and try to plan an original theme which fits into the syllabus. For example, knit a jersey and hat suitable for a very small, premature baby.
- Consider the important factors: the garment must be tiny, comfortable, lightweight not bulky, and not fluffy. It must be safe, with no holes in the pattern which fingers could catch in, no ribbons dangling, etc. The hat must fit well but not be too large.
- Take your knitting skills into account and keep your garments simple in style and pattern if you cannot knit well.
- Visit shops which sell knitting patterns and yarns. Make your choice considering all the important factors above, plus washability and cost.
- Begin your file, which will explain your working brief, the reasons for choice and selection of pattern and yarn, points you have considered, a drawing of the finished garment, construction of the garment, samples of yarn chosen, buttons to be used, etc.

Execution

- Carry out your working brief according to your original planning. Should you need to adapt your plan, note the alterations in your file and give reasons: for example, you may find the yarn too fluffy or harsh, the needle size may be too big, the garment may be working out too large, etc.

Assessment and evaluation

- When you have finished the garment, set yourself a questionnaire, which should include:
    Did I make a good choice of garment, yarn, pattern, etc.?
    Does the garment look and feel attractive?
    Will it serve the purpose stated in the working brief?
    Could it be improved, and if so how?
- If possible allow a baby to wear the garments for a short time. You can then efficiently judge their success. Do they fit? Are they safe? Are they comfortable? Do they wash well?
- Could you follow this work by making a matching pair of trousers? When the baby grows, is there any way of lengthening the jumper, or could you pull it out and use the yarn again for something else?
    All this information should go in your file. Try to keep a photographic record of your garments as you are making them, and a photograph of a baby wearing them. If you cannot photograph them, then draw each stage.

Birth and postnatal care (page 41)

Example 10.   New baby profile book (page 48)
The profile book should be kept as a loose-leaf folder and then additional material can be inserted. The new baby profile could begin with a collage of pictures of new babies (see page 58) or illustrations of how babies can look immediately after birth and then a few days later. For example, immediately after birth a baby's body may be covered in thick down, the soft bones of the skull may become elongated or the newborn baby may look skinny and wrinkled. These characteristics disappear within a few days.

Complete this with a brief written description of the baby's physical characteristics, for example, weight, height, head measurement, nails, hair, eye colour, body proportions, etc. The next page of your profile could deal with the natural reflexes of the newborn, with drawings and explanations as in the example below.

Then describe the physical and emotional needs of the new baby.

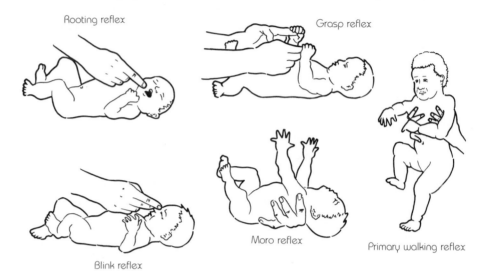

Rooting reflex

Grasp reflex

Blink reflex

Moro reflex

Primary walking reflex

Natural reflexes of the newborn baby

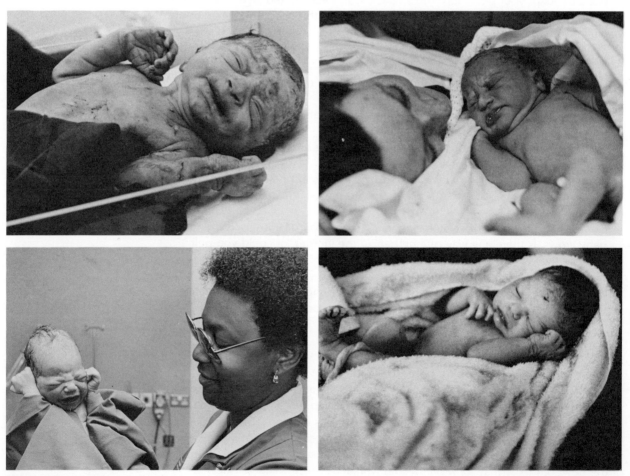

Appearance at birth

Example 11.   Bottle feeding (pages 45, 50)
Practical assignment: make up a bottle feed for a four-week-old baby.

Preparation Collect together:
1. A kettle to boil the water.
2. A sterilised feeding bottle, teat, measuring scoop, flat-bladed knife, infant formula milk powder.
3. Read the instructions on the box of milk powder to check the recommended amounts and instructions for making up.
4. Wash your hands.

Method used for preparing the feed:

Complete this assignment sheet and conclude by describing how to test the temperature of the milk and how to clean the bottle, teat and equipment after use.

Resources guide

Responsibilities for parenthood

Leaflets and booklets	**Publisher or source**
Predictor booklets, 'Preconceptual Care', 'Guide to a Healthy Pregnancy', etc.	Chefaro Proprietaries
Family Doctor booklet, 'Getting Fit for a Baby'	British Medical Association (BMA)
Leaflets on drugs, AIDS, smoking, alcohol	Department of Health, Health Education Council
Leaflets, 'Smoking, Alcohol, Drugs – Basic Facts'	Tacade
Nutrition leaflets and booklets	Sainsbury, Tesco
'Looking after yourself'	Health Education Council
'Prevent Air Pollution', 'Lead and you', etc.	National Society for Clean Air

Biological background

Leaflets, teaching packs, etc.	**Publisher or source**
'Look at Your Body', wallchart	Brook Advisory Service
'Male and Female', teaching cards about reproduction (also other resources)	Family Planning Association
'Very Personally Yours', about menstruation, for 9–15-year-olds. Mother and daughter packs	Simplicity Product Advisory Service
'It Happens to Us All', teaching kit	Johnson and Johnson Schools Information Service
Lecture service, booklets, product samples	Tampax Education Department
Speakers on all aspects of pregnancy and birth	The National Childbirth Trust
'A New Life', flip-over boards, teaching aid	Cow and Gate
'My Body'	Health Education Council
'Pregnancy to Birth'	Family Doctor Publications

'Timmy and Vicky', two interlinked plays to help with puberty problems

BBC Schools Broadcasts

'Development of the Embryo', 'Two Become One'

EFVA National Audio Visual Aids Library

Pregnancy

Cassette
Glad-to-be a Dad-to-be

Publisher or source
W Midlands Health Authority

Films
Maternity Hospital Routine
Ladies in Waiting

EVVA, National Audio Visual Aids Library (films to hire)

The New Good Birth Guide, S. Kitzinger

Palace Video, distributed by Palace and Virgin Distribution (WH Smith, Boots, etc.)

Leaflets and booklets
'Antenatal care' and other leaflets

Sterling Health

Pregnancy care card and pregnancy book, 'Rubella – The Facts'

Health Education Council

Leaflets about rubella

The National Rubella Council

'Guide to a healthy pregnancy'

Predictor

'What Every Mum and Dad should know about BSI'

British Standards Institute

Mothercare catalogue

Branches of Mothercare

Baby Boots catalogue

Branches of Boots the Chemist

Catalogue of children's wear and equipment

Oh/One/Oh

'Hopscotch', babies' and children's wear catalogue

Harrington's Nursery Collection

Magazines
Practical Parenting, Good Housekeeping, Family Matters

Birth and postnatal care

Film
Labour and Delivery, A Child is Born

Publisher or source
National Audio Visual Aids Library

Film strip or slide set
How Babies are Born

Focal Point Audio Visual Ltd

Leaflets and booklets
'How a Baby is Born' and other leaflets, 'When You've Had Your Baby'

Health Education Council

'Safer Pregnancy and Childbirth'

HMSO

'Post Natal Exercises'

Guild of Health Education Officers

'Eight Methods of Birth Control' and other leaflets

The Family Planning Information Services

Audio cassette

I Never Told a Soul, audio cassette,   Brook Advisory Centres
selection of other relevant material

Information can also be obtained from the following organisations:
National Childbirth Trust
Association for Improvements in the Maternity Services
The Birth Centre
La Leche League
Community Health Group for Ethnic Minorities
Caesarean Support Groups
Twins Clubs Association
The Foundation for the Study of Infant Deaths
Brook Advisory Centres, local centre in telephone directory.
Addresses are on page 159.

Books

	Publisher
Maternity Rights Handbook, R. Evans and L. Durward	Penguin
You and Your Child, S. Goodman	Galley Press
Being Born, S. Kitzinger	Dorling Kindersley
Biology in Action, D. Luxton	Blackie
Childbirth without Fear, G. Dick Read	Harper and Rowe Ltd
A First Home Economics Course, V. Reynolds and G. Wallace	Stanley Thornes (Publishers) Ltd
Baby and Co. Pregnancy and Birth Handbook, Dr M. Stoppard	Dorling Kindersley
Having a Baby, Dr M. Thom	Octopus Paperbacks
Pregnancy and Birth, S. Dale Tunnicliffe	Stanley Thornes (Publishers) Ltd
Learning to Care in the Community, P. Turton and J. Orr	Hodder and Stoughton
A New Life – A Comprehensive Guide	Marshall Cavendish
The Complete Book of Babycare	St Michael (Marks and Spencer)
Reader's Digest Mothercare Book	Hodder and Stoughton
The First Years of Life	Open University/Health Education Council

Development

UNIT ONE

Physical Development

Core information ―――――――――――

A child will develop rapidly during the early years of growth. This development can be divided into four areas, or types of development, but all of the areas are interlinked and dependent upon each other.

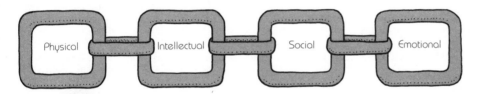

Physical — Intellectual — Social — Emotional

Types of development

Children all develop at their own rate, so only an average age can be given for each achievement or milestone. There is, however, a recognised pattern for each stage of development, which does not vary.

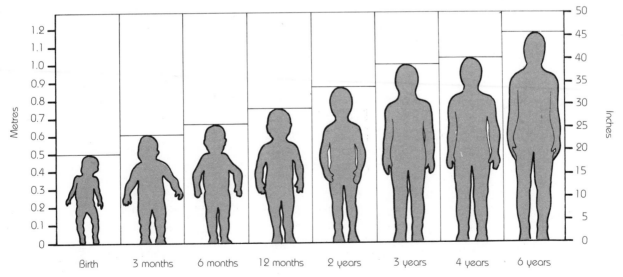

Body proportions and height – girls

Physical growth

At birth, a baby's head is one quarter of the total length; at six years it is one sixth of the total length and by adulthood it is one eighth of the total length. The limbs and the neck lengthen as the baby's chubbiness is lost. Eventually, weight, height and body shape will depend upon:

● diet   ● ethnic group   ● heredity   ● health.

Weight

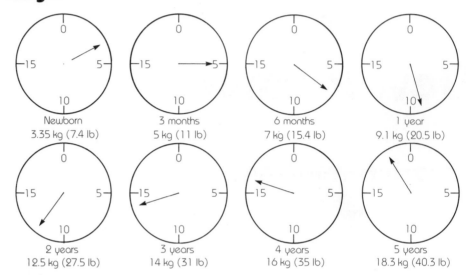

Newborn	3 months	6 months	1 year
3.35 kg (7.4 lb)	5 kg (11 lb)	7 kg (15.4 lb)	9.1 kg (20.5 lb)

2 years	3 years	4 years	5 years
12.5 kg (27.5 lb)	14 kg (31 lb)	16 kg (35 lb)	18.3 kg (40.3 lb)

Weight progress – girls

A newborn baby will lose a few grams in weight during the first few days. The baby will then almost double the birth weight in the first six months. Weight gain then slows down.

Teeth

There are 20 teeth in the first set, which are called milk teeth.

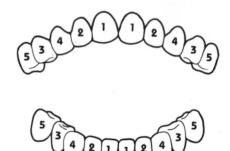

Teeth	Usually appear
Lower and upper front incisors	6–8 months
Lateral incisors	One year
First molars	18 months
Canines	18–20 months
Second molars	24–6 months

Major motor skills

The major motor skills include:

- sitting
- crawling
- standing
- walking
- kicking
- skipping
- running
- hopping
- climbing.

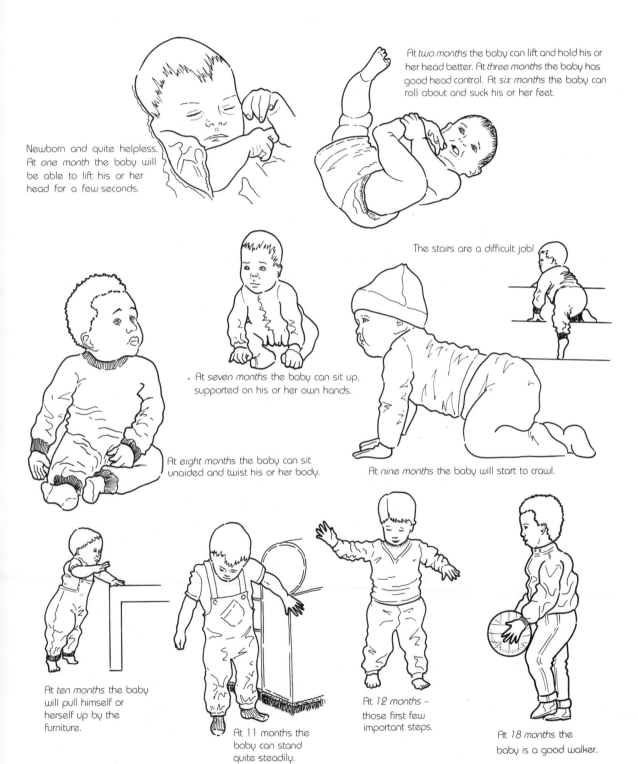

Newborn and quite helpless. At *one month* the baby will be able to lift his or her head for a few seconds.

At *two months* the baby can lift and hold his or her head better. At *three months* the baby has good head control. At *six months* the baby can roll about and suck his or her feet.

. At *seven months* the baby can sit up, supported on his or her own hands.

At *eight months* the baby can sit unaided and twist his or her body.

The stairs are a difficult job!

At *nine months* the baby will start to crawl.

At *ten months* the baby will pull himself or herself up by the furniture.

At 11 months the baby can stand quite steadily.

At *12 months* – those first few important steps.

At *18 months* the baby is a good walker.

Mobility milestones

18 months

Can get up and down stairs, climb up on a chair, walks very well, squats down to pick up a toy

2 years

Can run and stop, walk backwards, pull a wheeled toy, kick a ball and pick things up without falling over

2½ years

Can balance on tiptoe, pedal a tricycle, jump in the air and on and off things

3 years

Can balance on one foot, jump, climb, swing, walk on tiptoe

4 years

Will try to climb ladders and trees. Places one foot on each step when walking downstairs

5 years

Can skip with both feet, hop, walk on a narrow ledge, stand steadily on one leg, is very active

Major motor skills

Fine motor skills

The fine motor skills include manipulative skills involving coordination:
- reaching
- grasping
- holding
- releasing
- picking up
- placing.

Manipulative milestones

At **birth** and for the first few weeks, the hands are tightly clenched.
By **two months**, the hands are loosely open.
By **three months**, the hands stay open and the baby can grasp a rattle for short periods.
By **five months**, the baby can grasp objects with both hands.
By **six months**, the baby can awkwardly grasp a cube (primitive pincer grasp).
At **nine months**, picking up a small object between finger and thumb (mature pincer grip) is possible. The baby begins to use the index finger to poke into things.
At **twelve months**, the baby can hold a crayon in a fist, can place one brick on top of another, will release objects voluntarily and throw things from the pram.

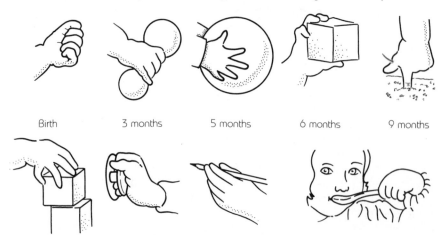

Birth   3 months   5 months   6 months   9 months

Manipulative milestones   12 months   2 years   2½ years   3 years

Fine skills progress more slowly during the second year.
At **15 months**, the baby can build a two-brick tower, hold two objects in one hand, take off shoes.
At **18 months**, the baby can scribble on paper, turn two or three pages of a book, take off shoes and socks.
At **2 years**, the baby can turn a door knob and unscrew lids, build a tower of six or seven bricks, wash and dry hands, and is now clearly left- or right-handed.
At **2½ years**, the child can take off trousers and pants, hold a pencil in the hand instead of the fist and start to scribble.
By **3 years**, the child can dress and undress, fasten buttons and zips, clean teeth, draw, colour, use scissors, and eat with a spoon and fork.

Over the next two or three years, the child's manipulative skills will, with the correct environmental stimulation, continue to increase until the fine skills required for basic independence have been acquired.

Drawing and painting involve the use of manipulative skills and are good practice for writing and other fine motor skills. The illustration shows the usual sequence in which a child learns.

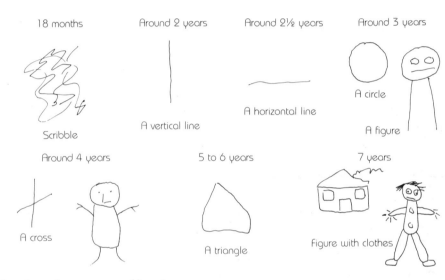

Drawing – the sequence of learning

Sensory development

We have five senses. They are:

● sight   ● hearing   ● touch   ● taste   ● smell.

1. **Vision and hand/eye coordination** The eyes of the newborn infant are usually closed, but the baby will: react to light – the pupils will dilate; turn the head towards a light which falls on one side of the face; blink at a sudden noise. Unable to focus the eyes together, the baby may appear to squint.
After a few weeks, the baby will: stare at a source of light; gaze at the mother's (or carer's) face; watch a toy move from side to side.
At six weeks old, the baby will: smile at the mother or carer when he or she comes into view; follow a moving person with the eyes.
At eight weeks, the baby's eyes are better able to focus.
By six months, the baby will: watch his or her hands move about; make both eyes converge; turn the head to follow a sound; recognise the feeding bottle; reach out to grasp a toy or object.

By six months, the baby likes to be propped up to watch moving people, trees, washing on the line, etc., and will be able to reach for and grasp objects easily. The eyes now move together and there should be no squint. Hand and eye movements should now coordinate to enable any object to be picked up. At 12 months, the baby can see and pick up small objects, watch and point at moving objects and look for things which are out of sight.

By the age of 2 years, almost perfectly formed vision has been achieved, although binocular vision and perception of depth are not fully developed until about 6 years of age.

2. **Hearing** Most newborn babies react to sound. They may cry, blink or go quiet when startled by a sudden noise. After a few weeks the baby will show fear of loud, sudden noises and respond to a comforting voice. By 3–4 months, the baby will turn the head towards a sound, show pleasure at mother's or carer's voice, cry or turn away from troublesome sounds. By 6 months, the baby can select some noises from others, for example, a parent's or carer's voice, and will respond with babbling and cooing sounds. By 9–12 months, the baby can respond to his or her own name, listen for particular sounds and voices and imitate sounds. A few words and simple commands can be understood. At this stage, hearing tests can be performed and signs of deafness identified.

3. The other senses are also present at birth and a baby soon learns to distinguish the particular **smell** of mother or carer. There is awareness of the sensation of **touch** and the pleasure of physical contact with the mother when she holds the baby close after birth. A sense of **taste** will begin to develop when the baby is introduced to different foods at a few months old.

These five senses develop naturally, but can all be encouraged through stimulation.

Physical care

For healthy physical development a high standard of care is needed. A child will need:

- healthy food and drink
- warmth and appropriate clothing
- fresh air, exercise and sleep
- a cleanliness routine.

Food and drink

Mixed feeding, or 'weaning', begins when the baby is ready for it, usually at about four months, or when the weight is between 6 and 7 kg (14 and 15 lb).

Basic rules to follow include:

- Do not start mixed feeding too early. It can make a baby overweight and the digestive system may not be able to cope.
- Introduce the first solids at breakfast or lunch-time feeds, but do not force them. If they are refused, try again later.
- Start with baby rice mixed with a little breast milk or baby formula milk.
- Introduce one new food at a time.
- Keep mealtimes calm and relaxed and do not get upset if the baby refuses food.
- Continue with early morning and evening milk feeds until the baby is 7 or 8 months old.
- Smooth puréed foods must be given until the baby is 6 months old. Food should then be minced or mashed until the baby can cope with biting and chewing.

- As well as milk feeds, a child should be given plain, boiled water, fresh fruit juice and good commercial juices.
- Try not to fuss over a child's diet as this can cause food faddiness.

Commercially prepared baby foods in cans or bottles, and dried foods are very useful: ● when the baby only requires small quantities ● if the mother (or carer) is unwell ● if parents are extra busy ● if someone else is looking after the baby ● if there is difficulty obtaining fresh foods ● if the family is away from home.

Freshly prepared foods, however, are often cheaper, and may be more nutritious and satisfying if well prepared and well cooked.

By the time a child is one year old he or she should be eating similar meals to the rest of the family. The baby will require a balanced diet with plenty of protein foods for body building, vitamins and minerals for protection against illness and to help the development of healthy blood, bones and body functions, and carbohydrates to provide warmth and energy.

Foods containing gluten · Egg white · Dried fruit · Cow's milk · Fruit squash · Cakes · Biscuits · Chocolate · Sweets · Ice-cream · Crisps · Salted peanuts · Bacon · Commercial foods containing high proportions of additives

Foods to avoid up to six months

Suggestions for clothing

Remember that most children are active, messy and unaware of danger, so their clothing should be:

- comfortable
- easy to put on and off
- not too fussy
- sturdy
- easily cleaned and laundered
- as safe as possible.

Outerwear   Items/points to look for include: warm lining, sturdiness, easy fitting, hood, good pockets, hem tie; thick cotton fabric for easy wash, no neck strings or surplus decoration which can be dangerous; PVC rain-jacket with hood, bright colour, easy press-stud fasteners; PVC boots with 'Day-glo' finish to be easily seen, comfortable trainers; cotton, well-fitting socks.

Playwear   Items/points to look for include: fleecy-backed, cotton, jogging pants and tops – easy wash, comfortable, protective, easy to put on and off, inexpensive; sturdy denim dungarees, cotton or cotton and polyester shirts, T-shirts, skirts, need little ironing, comfortable to wear; slip on, washable; play shoes with good grip sole.

Nightwear   Items/points to look for include: fleecy-lined cotton pyjamas, warm and cosy; cool cotton nightdresses for summer; all must be low-flammability; slip on, washable cheerful slippers.

Underwear   Items/points to look for include: cotton vests, pants, knickers, will take a hot wash, need no ironing, are cheap and attractive.

Warmth

Small children are the most at risk of hypothermia, which occurs when the body temperature falls below 32 °C (89.6 °F). Newborn babies are most at risk. Precautions to take are:

- If a baby is put outside in the pram in winter, warm the pram with a hot-water bottle and cover the baby with lightweight blankets, well tucked in. See that the baby has warm clothing and wears mittens, bootees and a hat.
- In winter the child's room should have, if possible, a constant night-time temperature of at least 18 °C (65 °F).
- Give the child a healthy diet with sufficient high-energy foods and warm drinks.
- Look for warning signs such as over-red cheeks, red and swollen hands and feet, being very cold to the touch, limpness and listlessness.

Fresh air, exercise and sleep

Children need fresh air and exercise to encourage them to be active, alert and healthy. These things will help to develop muscles, heart and lungs and assist in general development; the sun's rays on the body help to form vitamin D and aid healing processes.

The air in crowded urban areas is often polluted with petrol fumes, industrial waste and smoke, and children who live in these areas will benefit from being taken to parks and play areas and making visits to the countryside and seaside.

Even in cold weather, babies and small children can be well wrapped up and left outside in the pram to sleep or taken to play, but fog should be avoided. Fresh air and exercise during the day will help children's appetites and also help them to relax and sleep. Children vary in the amounts of sleep they require. The chart indicates average amounts, but it will depend upon the child's temperament, state of health, surroundings and day-time activity.

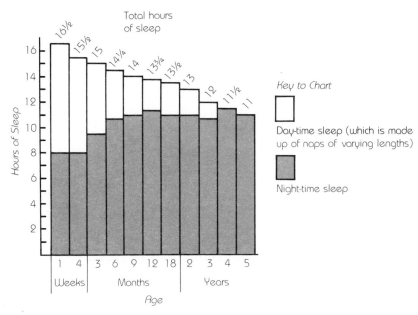

Total hours of sleep

Key to Chart

Day-time sleep (which is made up of naps of varying lengths)

Night-time sleep

Typical amounts of sleep needed during childhood

Conditions which encourage sound sleep are:

- A quiet time before bedtime with a bedtime story.
- Warm or cool bedclothes – not too heavy.
- Comfortable mattress; use a pillow only after one year.
- Comfortable nightwear.
- Warm or cool room, small amount of fresh air, no draughts.
- Leaving a favourite toy or comforter and a dummy if necessary.
- Leaving a small light on and the bedroom door ajar if required.
- Giving kind but firm treatment to children who can't or won't settle down.

Cleanliness and hygiene

A hygiene routine should be established as soon as the child can understand simple instructions. Personal skills will become automatic within a short time if:

- rules are simple and easy to follow   ● suitable items are provided, for example, hot water, soap, toothbrush, clean towels, etc.   ● all the family provide a good example   ● there are constant reminders   ● rewards are given for good effort.

By the time school age is reached, the child should be able to care for skin, hair, nails and teeth with limited supervision and realise the reasons why this needs to be done:

- It is part of becoming socially acceptable.
- Lack of hygiene can lead to infections and disease.

Toilet training

There is no set age for bowel and bladder control. A child will achieve this when ready and cannot be rushed. Encouragement can be given by:

- Parents remaining calm and encouraging, not getting worried and trying to rush the process.
- Choosing the right moment to start.
- Giving praise and rewards.
- Providing a well-designed, attractive potty and allowing the child to get used to it.
- Giving confidence by using a child-size lavatory seat and a foot stool.

Bowel control usually comes first by the time the child is between 15 and 18 months old, bladder control during the day by 2–2½ years.

Most children are toilet trained by the age of 3 years, but it can take longer.

Children may regress if they are:

● ill   ● unhappy   ● emotionally disturbed   ● frightened   ● away from home   ● too busy to bother.

If a child is soiling pants at 4 years and still wetting at 5 years, parents should seek professional guidance.

Protection from disease

There are many common ailments in childhood, the most usual being the infectious diseases. Most of them clear up quickly, but they should not be neglected or they may become serious. Many infections can be prevented by:

● paying attention to hygiene   ● avoiding contact with the infection   ● having a balanced, healthy diet   ● regular checkups   ● adequate warmth and protection   ● immunisation.

Some common childhood ailments are: asthma, bronchitis, croup, colds and influenza, coughs, conjunctivitis, earache, tummy upsets, eczema and allergic conditions, convulsions and thrush.

Many of these respond to warmth, rest, fluids, modified diets and simple home remedies. For severe cases, help may be obtained from child clinics, health visitor, chemist or doctor.

Signs of illness include: being pale, listless, hot and feverish; poor appetite; irritability; high temperature; vomiting; swollen glands; aches and pains; crying and poor breathing.

A child's temperature may be taken by using one of the thermometers illustrated below.

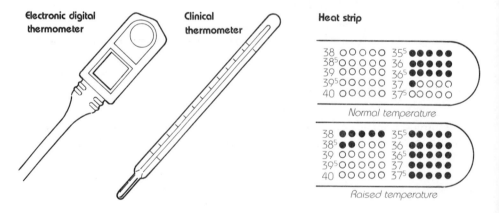

Electronic digital thermometer   Clinical thermometer   Heat strip

Normal temperature

Raised temperature

Infectious diseases

● Immunisation will help to protect most children from infectious diseases (IDs).
● There is much more risk of death or permanent damage from diseases than from their vaccines.
● If a child does catch a disease after immunisation, it should be in a much milder form.
● Every child immunised also reduces the risks to others. Some IDs have been almost eradicated because of the immunisation programme.
● Immunisation is free and will be carried out at a clinic or doctor's surgery.

Parents should keep a record of when these vaccinations have been given. Immunisation should be postponed and the doctor consulted if the child:

- is feverish, with a high temperature
- is epileptic
- has any allergies
- is taking medication
- is generally unwell.

A safe environment

The under-fives are almost totally unaware of danger. As their physical development progresses, they are able to pick things up, put things in their mouths, climb, become mobile, run and dart about; they become more daring and adventurous.

Until they can understand the relationship between situations and danger, parents must make their environment as accident free as possible and also teach and reinforce safety skills. In the home each year there are approximately 5900 fatal accidents and 3 188 000 non-fatal accidents. Elderly people are the most susceptible to fatal accidents, but 4 per cent of fatal accidents happen to the under-fives.

Young children are the most susceptible to non-fatal accidents. 23 per cent of non-fatal accidents happen to the under-fives.

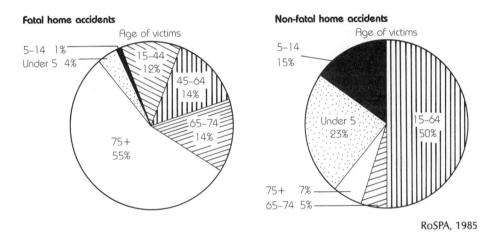

Fatal home accidents

Age of victims

5–14 1%
Under 5 4%
15–44 12%
45–64 14%
65–74 14%
75+ 55%

Non-fatal home accidents

Age of victims

5–14 15%
Under 5 23%
15–64 50%
75+ 7%
65–74 5%

RoSPA, 1985

The most dangerous places in the home for the under-fives are shown below. (Numbers given represent the number of accidents to under-fives in that part of the house in a year.)

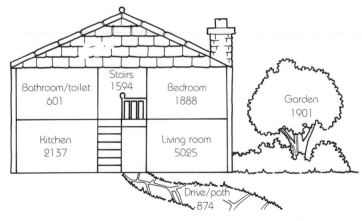

Bathroom/toilet 601
Stairs 1594
Bedroom 1888
Garden 1901
Kitchen 2137
Living room 5025
Drive/path 874

Department of Trade and Industry, 1988

The most common types of home accident to children are:

Falls from windows, downstairs, etc.: 94 000 falls downstairs and 1500 falls from windows each year in the 0–14 age group.

Accidental poisoning: usually from household products and medicines.

Cuts: often caused by breakages of glass in doors and windows.

Burns: fires, often started by open fires or matches, cause about 100 child deaths a year.

Scalds: caused by spillage from kettles, or cups of hot liquid.

Bruising: caused by falls, or as the result of abuse by another person.

Many products may be so badly designed or carelessly used that they cause accidents. These are some of the worst offenders (England and Wales):

Article	No. of accidents caused in 1986	Article	No. of accidents caused in 1986
Cot/bed	116	Bleach	145
High chair	135	Swings	262
Baby/safety gate	112	Balls	369
Pram	128	Dolls/soft toys	53
Baby walker	238	Tricycles	105
Baby's dummy	14	Baby's bottle	40

Many of these accidents can be prevented if:

● young children are constantly supervised ● children are taught safety facts ● good examples are given ● government safety regulations are enforced ● houses are designed for safety ● goods are bought with safety in mind ● safety equipment is used ● constant checks are kept on equipment ● everyone takes **care**.

Dealing with an accident

General points are:

● Have a first-aid box and know where it is – keep the contents up to date.
● Get to know how to deal with all types of accidents and take a first-aid course if possible.
● Do not panic if an accident occurs, but act promptly and calmly.
● Remove the source of danger, for example, switch off electric current.
● Try to stop the flow if there is heavy bleeding.
● If the child has taken a poisonous substance, keep some of it to show the doctor.
● If you do not know the correct first-aid procedure and the child is still breathing and not bleeding heavily, do nothing and get help quickly.
● Try not to leave the child.
● Keep the child warm, but do not give food or drink.
● Even if the injury only appears mild, take the child to have it checked.

Road safety

Young children are the most at risk when it comes to accidents on the road. In a survey quite a high proportion of mothers believed that a 3-year old was safe on the road alone. A child is well over the age of 5 before being able to assess the speed of cars and appreciate other road dangers. Until then, children need supervision. In another survey it was discovered that six out of ten under-fives injured in road accidents were less than 100 m from home. In Great Britain on average 500 children are killed in road accidents each year and 50 000 children are injured in road accidents each year.

Join the Tufty Club.

Accompany the child cyclist.

Explain the hazards.

Use the Green Cross Code.

Use reins in the early years.

Let the child wear luminous discs, 'Day-glo' arm bands, fluorescent jacket and shoes.

Hold the child's hand firmly.

Ways of achieving road safety

Safety in cars

The law states that drivers and front-seat passengers must wear a suitably approved restraint. Child restraints should have a kitemark.

It is recommended that children should travel in the rear seats. Suitable child restraints should be used to suit the age and size of the child, such as carry-cot restraints; rear-facing restraints; child safety seats and harnesses; and booster cushions. They should all be securely held in place.

Other areas of danger include play parks and recreation grounds, areas of water such as ponds, rivers, canals and swimming pools and the beach. Constant supervision is essential.

Play

Play is an essential part of childhood. It is the way in which children learn and it is necessary for all the developmental areas.

Within the area of physical development, play will encourage:
- muscular coordination
- hand–eye coordination
- manipulative skills
- mobility
- balance
- manual dexterity
- sensory skills.

Stages of play development

Approximate age	Type of play
Up to 4 or 5 months	*Exploratory play.* The young baby observes surroundings, stretches, kicks and may reach out to try to grasp a finger or a rattle; as coordination improves he or she will grasp things and explore them with the mouth.
Up to 18 months or 2 years	*Solitary play.* The child enjoys playing alone, but with the mother or another adult within sight.
2–3 years	*Parallel play.* Children like to play alongside other children but do not play with them in a cooperative way.
Over 3 years	*Group play.* Children play together, learning how to share and get along socially.

Older children still enjoy solitary and parallel play and should be given opportunities for these.

The child will learn better and more quickly if play is fun. Objects and activities to stimulate and interest are needed. Toys and activities become the learning tools and they must therefore:

- Be suitable for the level of ability. A recommended age range for a toy is only a general guide.
- Look exciting, be colourful and attractive.
- Be neither too simple nor too complex. A toy which is too simple becomes boring and an over-complicated one can be frustrating.
- Provide something to do and offer a challenge.
- Offer opportunities for discovery and the acquisition of new skills.

When purchasing toys it is necessary to consider:

- Design. They should be sturdy, well made and suitable for their purpose.
- Safety. Toys must be safe and comply with government safety regulations.
- Cost. Expensive toys are not necessarily good toys, but some cheap toys are badly made and unsafe, and do not last.
- Hygiene. All toys should be cleanable.

Approximate age	Appropriate toys
Up to 6 months	Choose toys to encourage eye movement, listening, aiming and grasping, such as teething rings, a musical mobile, soft toys to grip.
6–12 months	Choose toys to encourage hand movements, hand–eye coordination and exploring with hand and mouth, such as bell rattle, activity bear, pull-along toys.
1–2 years	Choose toys to encourage fine motor skills, balance and mobility, such as building blocks, peg and hammer.
2–5 years	Choose toys to encourage and develop all physical skills, such as construction toys, threading games, posting box.

Pupil participation

Working briefs

1. Development

Individual work (Investigation)

To study the physical development of very young children you could try one of these:

- Visit a council nursery which looks after young babies.
- Study a child whom you know from the age of 2 months to 18 months.
- Invite some mothers or carers with young babies to come in to your school a few times.

You can then complete an observation sheet like the one below. Compare the rate of progress of boys and girls, if possible.

Comparative Observational Study	Mobility		Date: From	To
Child's Name(s)		Age		
Activity	Boy	Girl	Comments	
Holds head up for a few seconds			Was the child's mobility influenced by his or her weight?	
Good head control				
Rolls from tummy on to back				
Lies on back and grasps foot			Did any minor illness slow down the rate of progress?	
Holds head firmly erect				
Sits up without support				
Attempts to crawl			Can children be helped if they are given encouragement?	
Crawls purposefully				
Pulls himself or herself up with the aid of furniture				
Walks with hand(s) held			Do boys progress more or less quickly than girls?	
Walks unaided				
Walks well				

Further developmental charts can be made to observe hand–eye coordination, manipulative skills, etc.

2. Personal skills

Varied group work

It is important that personal skills such as washing, dressing, feeding, going to the toilet, etc., are learned as soon as possible so that the child is well prepared for school life.

Divide into three groups:

Group 1 Design a small booklet listing all the personal skills which an under-five should acquire and give suggestions for teaching and reinforcing these skills, such as teaching by example. Illustrate your book.

Group 2 Make some straightforward teaching aids to help a child learn about care of the teeth, toilet hygiene, dressing, etc. You could make a book, an activity learning toy or a bedroom frieze.

Group 3 Make a fabric wall collage showing the different fasteners which can be used on children's clothing, and which are simple for a child to manipulate, for example, Velcro strips, chunky zips, toggle fasteners and large buttons.

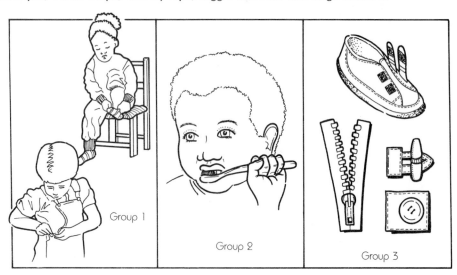

When you have completed your assignments, have a class discussion to evaluate your work.

3. Food
Class work (Problem solving)

These pictures start a story which can happen in any family
a) Complete the picture strip (in drawings or in words) to show how the situation should be dealt with.
b) Explain why the method shown in pictures two and three is wrong.

Once upon a time . . .

'I'm not hungry . . . this time. I'll eat more next time she brings it . . .'

'He's not eating! He'll get ill! He must eat! I'll have to coax him . . .'

'Please, for mummy! To please me! You must take it . . . I'll tell you a story . . . please . . .'

4. Clothing
Problem-solving assignment

Bring to school an item of children's clothing which is badly worn or outgrown. The item could be:

● a pinafore dress with torn pockets   ● dungarees with worn-out knees and the straps too short   ● tracksuit top and trousers which are outgrown.

Your brief is to give the garments extra life in an imaginative way. The suggestions below may help. If you cannot find a suitable garment, make up a book of practical ideas and suggestions for extending the life of outgrown children's clothing.

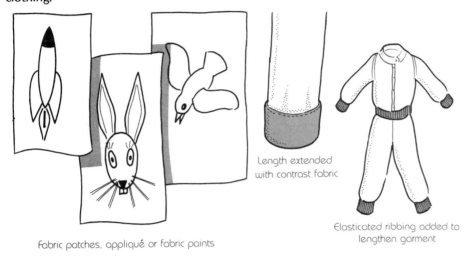

Length extended with contrast fabric

Elasticated ribbing added to lengthen garment

Fabric patches, appliqué or fabric paints

5. Safety

In the home   **Individual work (Quiz)**

Devise a quiz which will help to make parents of young children safety conscious. Prepare a leaflet to go with the quiz which gives a selection of safety aids available for the home, their cost, and where to obtain them.

(See example on page 105.)

On the road   **Individual work (Collaborative learning game)**

Make a game which you could play with a small child to teach them basic facts about road safety. The examples shown below are produced by RoSPA as part of their Tufty road safety scheme.

6. Caring for the sick child   Class discussion/Guest speaker

Children who are ill need special care. Divide into small groups to tackle this subject. Select one of the topics below and collect as much information as you can. Use case histories if possible.

a) When should the doctor be called? Which symptoms and conditions are serious and need a doctor to pay a home visit, and which can be treated sensibly by the child's parents?

b) Can you remember having an infectious disease? What are the symptoms for each infectious disease and what is the treatment?

c) Food and drink are important for the child who is ill. What factors should be considered when planning the diet of a child who is ill and one who is convalescing?

d) How can the child who is getting better be kept amused all day?

e) Going into hospital can be a traumatic experience for children. How can they be prepared beforehand?

When you have collected your information together, discuss the topics within the class. You may be able to invite a nurse from a children's hospital, or a health visitor, to speak to your group about looking after children who are ill.

7. Play and toys   Class work (fact file)

a) Safety. There are many cases of accidents caused by dangerous toys reported in newspapers and on TV. Keep a group fact file of these cases and at the end of each report suggest ways in which the accident could have been avoided. Find out what to do if you find a dangerous toy. Put this information in your file.

b) Make a toy or game for a baby or toddler which is designed with safety in mind. In the planning and execution of your work, highlight the various safety features. Use fabric, wood or card and make sure that you consider safety points such as:
   ● non-flammable fabric   ● strong, firm seams   ● non-toxic paint and stuffing   ● splinter-free finish   ● no projecting nails or sharp edges
   ● no small parts or decorations which a child could remove and swallow.

(See example on page 106.)

Written work

Fact finding exercise

1. Find out about and then write a paragraph on:
   feeding equipment for young children   potty training a young child
   choosing footwear for children   a toddler's sleep problems
   satisfactory methods of storing children's toys.

2. How would you deal with a toddler:
   a) Found with an empty bottle of bleach beside her?
   b) Bitten by a dog?
   c) Concussed after falling from his high chair?
   d) With a grazed knee?
   e) With a deep cut on her finger?

Application of knowledge

1. Sometimes small children do not like the flavour of fresh milk. Suggest several alternative ways in which it may be served in their diet.

2. Sometimes it is necessary to make food look exciting and appetising to tempt the child with a small appetite. The picture gives one suggestion – draw and describe some others.

Smiley pizza

3. How do the following affect tooth decay and dental care:
    - fluoride   ● regular cleaning   ● fruit acids   ● preventive dentistry
    - ice lollies and toffees   ● selecting a toothbrush?

4. Draw and label a first-aid tin and its contents.

Problem solving

What advice would you give to grandparents who were expecting their young grandchildren to stay, and wanted to make their home and garden safe?

Structured exercise

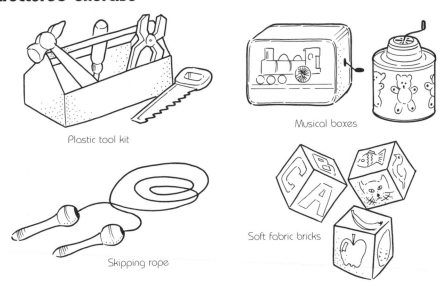

Plastic tool kit

Musical boxes

Skipping rope

Soft fabric bricks

1. For what age and stage of development are the above toys suitable?

2. What physical skills would each toy be helping to develop?

3. Approximately how much would each toy cost? Would it be good value for money?

4. What safety points would you look for before buying?

Free response

Explain how diet, ethnic group and heredity will affect the physical growth of a child.

81

Data response

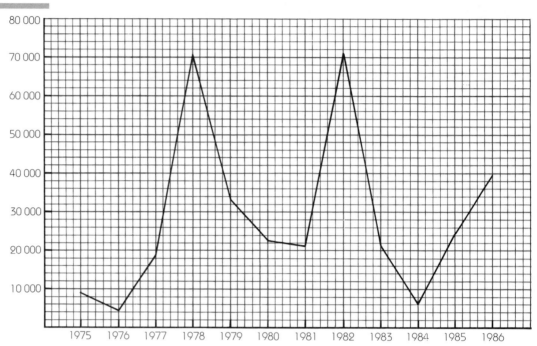

Number of cases of whooping cough in the UK

1. What is the highest number of whooping cough cases recorded and in which year do they occur?

2. How many years elapse between each peak in numbers?

3. In the mid- to late-1970s there was a scare linking immunisation with brain damage. What happens to the figures shown on the graph at this stage?

4. What are the symptoms of whooping cough? Why can it be so dangerous?

5. Write a paragraph about immunisation and its effects on such diseases as polio and tuberculosis.

Self-assessment

Photocopy and complete the self-assessment chart on page 161, inserting the following topics under 'The work I have done includes':

1. Physical growth
2. Development of:
   motor skills
   manipulative skills
   coordination
3. Sensory development
4. Health and hygiene
5. Protection from disease
6. Safety and first aid
7. Play, toys and games.

Photocopy and complete the self-marking plan on page 162 for the seven working briefs in this unit.

Intellectual Development

Core Information

Intellectual development is the growth of mental capacity and the ability to think. These develop into:

- The intellectual skills of speech and language.
- The concept of number.
- The ability to form and understand concepts and ideas.

As with physical development, the **sequence** of intellectual development is the same for all children; the **rate** of development may vary. A child's intellectual development can be seen in the progress made in acquiring physical skills and the awareness of and interest in the surrounding conditions. Intellectual development will be encouraged by the stimulation provided in a child's immediate environment.

Maturation rate and achievement of skills

The baby. Sensori-motor period (0–2 years)

Approximate age	General understanding	Communication and language skills
0–3 months	Experimental stage. The baby is learning through the senses. First gains knowledge of own body and then of external objects. Begins to link new experiences to old ones and make connections. A non-verbal stage, although there is communication in the form of eye contact, hand signs and noises.	Initially hand movements and lip and tongue movements (pre-speech stage) are used to communicate. Crying will indicate distress. The baby will turn head towards a sound source and by 3 months will smile and coo with pleasure.
6 months	Child will be reaching out for things, becoming mobile and wanting to explore. May be able to distinguish between some shapes. Will turn head in response to own name. Will learn by putting objects to the mouth to suck and to taste.	The baby will be able to recognise mother or a familiar figure. Will laugh and chuckle at what is seen or heard. Can put expression into vowel sounds such as 'a–a', and repeat two-syllable words, such as 'da–da'.

Approximate age	General understanding	Communication and language skills
9 months	Will realise that an object may still be there even if it cannot be seen. Will reach for things out of range and understand the meaning of 'no'. Still learning by trial and error.	Babbling is more meaningful. Will begin to imitate sounds and understands a few words, such as 'bye-bye'. May be able to say one word with meaning.
12 months	Enjoys repetitive play, nursery rhymes and simple books. Likes to make people laugh, memory is developing and the child is beginning to use reasoning processes. Is inquisitive and demanding.	Says two or three words with meaning, and understands many more; also understands simple commands, own name and words for familiar things. Is using most vowels and consonants.
18 months	Can scribble with a pencil and recognise pictures of things. Is becoming more independent and will try to use a comb and toothbrush. Will copy mother or father in domestic work and carry out simple instructions. Understands idea of toilet training. Is unaware of danger.	Child will use the correct word for an object and with understanding; uses 6–20 words and understands many more. Will join in with nursery rhymes and songs and jabbers freely.

The toddler. Pre-conceptual period (2–4 years)

2 years	Personality is developing, intelligence level will become apparent. Memory improves and he or she will remember people and objects. Realises he or she is a separate being and that things can be manipulated. Will be able to think through situations and realise consequences. Going through a negative phase. Involved in parallel play. Understands difference between 'one' and 'many'.	Uses 50 or more words, chatters incessantly. Uses words, 'I, me, you'; can use two or three words together in a simple sentence; will imitate tones of voice, repeat things and ask for food, toilet, etc. Talks to himself or herself in own language, listens to others, knows own name.
$2\frac{1}{2}$ years	Recognises basic numbers; can draw vertical and horizontal lines; is becoming less negative and more independent. Memory and attention span improving, also basic understanding of time. Becoming aware of quantity, weight and size and can identify many colours.	Uses 200 or more words, understands many more; knows full name and can repeat a simple nursery rhyme. Sentence construction still immature. Talks continuously during play and asks endless questions.

Approximate age	General understanding	Communication and language skills
3 years	May remember things from many months back, is constantly seeking out information and has an increasing span of concentration. Is aware of sexual differences. Likes games of pretend and is more sociable. Knows own age, has a good impression of depth and knows the difference between 'big' and 'little'.	Should have an extensive vocabulary, learning up to 50 new words a month, which can be used intelligently and grammatically. Can locate and name body parts. Carries on extended conversations, knows many rhymes and songs. Can describe activities.

The infant. Intuitive period (4–7 years)

4 years	Is aware of past, present and future time, and of the concepts of heavier, higher and longer. Attempts to reason, but may confuse cause and effect. Is still thinking intuitively, not logically. Can recognise and name eight to ten picture cards and count up to 20 with more understanding. Can concentrate on a book for quite long periods; can draw and identify common geometric shapes.	Speaks intelligibly, knows own name, age and address. Enjoys telling and hearing jokes and repeating nursery rhymes and songs. Can give long accounts of events, real or imaginary. Correct grammatical usage. May still have difficulty with 's–f–th' sound groups.

Over the remaining preschool years, intellectual development will progress rapidly. At 5 years, the child can usually speak fluently and grammatically, can count up to fifteen bricks, may be able to read and write a little and repeat a list of twelve words. Perception of size, colour and shape will be good.

Environmental stimulation

Satisfactory play situations will stimulate and develop memory, concentration, an appreciation of cause and effect, imagination, curiosity and the desire to learn. These learning processes will take place in the correct sequence, but progress may be encouraged and hastened by:

● a stimulating environment   ● good teaching and guidance   ● satisfactory model(s) to copy.

Important points to remember are:

● The child's home surroundings should be stimulating; for example, they should provide colour, pictures, books and things to watch and listen to.
● Opportunities for play should be provided and play should not be discouraged because it is messy.
● Playing with natural substances, such as sand, soil and water, will help a child to understand the surrounding world.
● A child should not be left alone for long periods to become bored and lonely.
● Communication is important, even before there appears to be any response.
● Special times for play should be set aside by working parents.

- The child's efforts should be rewarded with praise and approval and treated with interest.
- When at the stage of asking lots of questions, the child should be answered patiently and truthfully.
- Outside activities and visits are important to stimulate curiosity, reasoning and memory.
- Comparisons with other children who may appear more intellectually advanced can be misplaced and damage a child's confidence.
- Young children have only a short span of attention. Forcing them to concentrate for long periods or trying to teach intellectual skills beyond their abilities can be detrimental.
- A child's progress is controlled by 'nature and nurture'. Skills will be acquired at their own pace, but parents can seek expert advice if:

  The child can't convey meaning by 18 months old.
  Speech is not reasonably clear by $2\frac{1}{2}$–3 years.
  The child doesn't string words together by $2\frac{1}{2}$ years.
  Pictures in a book can't be named by 3 years.
  Adult actions are not imitated by 2 years.
  The child is unable to recognise three colours by the age of 4 years.

Toys and activities for intellectual development

Toy manufacturers produce hundreds of toys and games designed to help intellectual development. Many are good, but children will also learn from simple things going on around them.

Books for the under-fives:

The most valuable thing which a parent or carer can do to aid intellectual progress is to develop in a child an interest and a love of books. Many books are cheap when new, and they may be bought secondhand or borrowed from friends or from the public library. Once obtained, books should be used. Adults should read suitable poems and stories to their children and eventually encourage them to read for themselves. Public libraries often have story-telling sessions for the under-fives. Books will encourage all aspects of learning. They should be selected carefully:

- Rag books, board books and wipeable books are best for very young children.
- First books should be mainly pictures, with simple text, and should be colourful and short.
- Toddlers love action-filled books with repetitive sounds which they can join in saying. They enjoy rhymes and poems.
- Longer stories should be understandable to the child. Fantasy stories can stimulate a child's imagination but should not be too frightening.
- Children enjoy reading about their favourite TV characters.
- Instructive books, which teach road safety, how to cope with situations like going to the dentist, etc., can be useful.
- Activity books with pop-up pictures or musical squeaks, books which float, etc., will amuse the child.
- Stories and language beyond a child's understanding will just be boring and frustrating.
- Pictures should be bright, simple and relate to the story.
- Look to see if the book gives you an age guide.
- Story-telling requires skill. You should read quite slowly and carefully, pointing to the picture and involving the child as you go along.
- Teach a child to take care of books.
- Books which give stereotyped ideas of male and female roles or lifestyles, or contain cultural stereotypes, should be avoided.

Educational provision for the under-fives

Mother and toddler groups are usually set up on a voluntary basis. They consist of informal meetings for parents and children to socialise, but also provide a learning situation. There are toys, space and opportunities to be with other children. All these enlarge the child's horizon.

Playgroups are much more structured than mother and toddler groups. They are registered with the local authority, but largely funded and run by the parents themselves. Play groups:

- Are an excellent introduction to formal school life.
- Provide toys and facilities the child may not have access to at home.
- Allow children to mix at an age (3 years) when they are ready for cooperative play.
- Provide learning opportunities.
- Encourage independence and allow a short separation period for child and parent.
- Provide activities and games, under the guidance of a trained person, for the age range of the children.

A child that is unhappy at first should have a short break and start again when more ready for the experience.

Nursery schools may be state maintained or privately run. They are usually more formal than playgroups and may attempt more structured learning programmes.
Primary schools Education is compulsory from the age of 5 and primary schools accept children in their fifth year. The infants' section of a good primary school will be buzzing with activity, with children learning skills in many different ways. Some children begin at primary school with some literacy and numeracy skills, but it is more useful if they:

- Have been taught basic social skills, such as using the toilet, tying shoelaces and using a knife and fork.
- Have been allowed to make contact with other children and know how to share and be friendly.
- Are independent, secure and willing to leave home for a short time, knowing it will still be there on their return.

- Have a good command of language and know their name, address, age and phone number.
- Have often been read to and are accustomed to listening.
- Have enquiring minds.

Pupil participation

Working briefs

1. Achievement of skills

Individual work (Investigation)

It is possible that you are doing a child study as part of an examination course. Assess the progress made by the child you are studying and compare it with that expected of the 'average' child. For example:

Name of child: Jane Age: 2 years 4 months		Name of child: Mark Age: 3 years 6 months	
General understanding √ or X	Speech √ or X	General understanding √ or X	Speech √ or X
Does the child: Enjoy quiet play? Recognise three numbers? Draw horizontal lines? Identify two or more colours? Build up a four-cube tower? Scribble spontaneously? Remember from last week?	Does the child: Use more than 100 words? Know his or her name? Listen to other people? Repeat a nursery rhyme? Follow two instructions? Point to named body parts? Ask lots of questions?	Does the child: Like games of pretend? Recognise ten numbers? Draw and identify geometric shapes? Recognise ten picture cards? Build a complex construction? Concentrate on a book? Remember from many months ago?	Does the child: Know up to 500 words? Know name, age and address? Carry on a conversation? Repeat many songs and rhymes? Use correct grammar? Is the child finished with baby talk? Constantly seeking information?

Another study can then be made by comparing the standards achieved by the child you are studying with those achieved by a child who is approximately one year older.

2. Cause and effect

Group and class discussion

Divide into three groups to discuss the 'cause and effect' situations below, one group to each age group. Add to the 'causes' if you can. Decide what the 'effect' will be and possible reasons for it.

Get together with the rest of the class to discuss your findings.

Cause	Effect	√	Reasons
Young baby: 1. Hears sound of bottle being prepared.	The child smiles and gets excited or cries, or ignores it.		
2. Given rattle to play with, then rattle hidden under a cloth.	The child looks round for toy or lifts the cloth to find it or forgets about the object.		
Toddler: 1. Parent repeats a nursery rhyme every night to the child.	The child becomes bored with it, or joins in spontaneously, or demands rhyme repeatedly.		
2. Is given a toy beyond his or her level of skills.	The child becomes bored and rejects it, or screams with frustration, or tries to master it.		
4 or 5 years old: 1. Given a quite difficult puzzle to do.	The child will try to force it, or not attempt it, or think and then attempt it.		
2. At playgroup the child will . . .	Prefer to play alone, or prefer to play with an adult, or play with other children.		

This work may also be done as individual work by copying the chart into your book.

3. A child's environment   Class work (Brainstorming)

Take a short time to think about and research the following.

How can a small bedroom used by an under-five be made interesting and intellectually stimulating? Consider decoration, wall friezes, toy storage, scribbling space, etc. Look for ideas in books and magazines.
Get together a 'brainstorming' session. Consider everyone's contributions and then do a set of illustrated plans for children's bedrooms.

4. Stimulating activities   Problem-solving assignments

a) **Story building** Draw a set of four or five simple pictures which could be built into a story. If possible show the pictures to a child and get him or her to develop the story plan with you. Add short sentences to explain the pictures and make up a book together. The child will enjoy making the book with you and will have learnt a lot from you.

Story building

b) **Number** Make a colourful plan of a village or town. Make stand-up models to put on the plan, for example, three cars, four cows, six houses and five trees. Grouping these together will give a child the idea of number.

c) **Colour and shape** Cover some stiff card with felt. Divide the board into squares and label each one. Cut out suitable shapes in coloured felt to fit into each square. This will help a child to distinguish colour and shape.

When you have made your games, try them out with children of different ages. Evaluate your work – was it a good design? Could it be improved?

5. Speech development Individual work (Investigation)

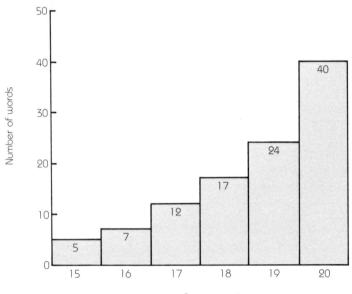

Age in months

This chart shows the progress made by an 'average' child during the first six months of talking. Try to listen to children of similar ages speaking. How many words do they use with meaning? How many more words do they understand?

This is a list of words most frequently used by small children:

dog	water	clock	apple
cat	bottle	boat	cake
shoe	duck	light	horse
milk	book	key	hat

Check the list with a young child you know. Which words did he or she understand first?

(See example on page 107.)

6. Preparation for primary school Class work (Rounds)

'To prepare a child for primary school I would . . .'

Take a few minutes to consider this and then go round the class with everyone making suggestions.
If possible, before this activity, watch a video showing young children at school, *or* visit an infant's school *or* ask a care assistant from a local infants school to come to describe his or her work.

Written work

Fact finding exercise

1. Find out about and write a paragraph on each of the following: Professor Jean Piaget, the Swiss psychologist; toy libraries; the Pre-school Playgroups Association.

2. Compare and explain: Nature   and nurture.
                         Sequence   and rate of development.
                         Speech   and language.

Application of knowledge

1. Explain the terms: concepts; maturation; cognitive development; environment; stimulation; vocabulary.

2. How would you deal with the following problems?
   a) Errol is 3 years old but is not yet making much progress with his speech and his parents are worried. He has two older siblings.

      Suggest some possible reasons for this slowness. What can his parents do to help his progress? Where could the child's parents go for advice and who can help them?

   b) Susan is shy and timid and does not mix well. Her parents want to boost her confidence and independence before she starts primary school.

      How can they prepare the child? What activities could she become involved in? How would it help if they all visited the school beforehand?

Free response

The mother and baby in the photograph are communicating. Describe how communication takes place, through all the senses, in the first few weeks of life.

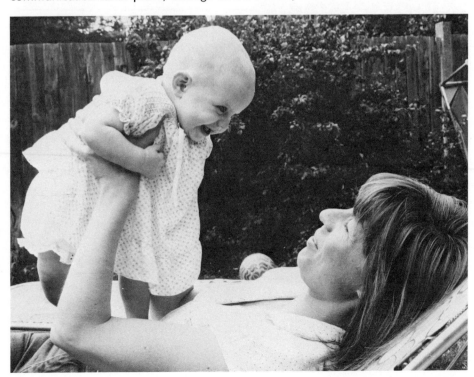

Data response

B — Could understand the idea of 'All gone' and 'More' . . .

D — Recognised herself in a mirror . . .

E — Got excited at the prospect of a feed . . .

A — Discovered he could move a toy by pulling its string . . .

C — Made two-syllable sounds . . .

1. Put the milestones shown above in the correct developmental sequence.

2. How will the children in pictures B, D and E react to the situations they are in?

3. How can the skills shown in the pictures be reinforced and encouraged by the children's parents?

4. From your own experience of studying children, give a brief profile of a 1-, 2- or 3-year-old child, with special emphasis given to intellectual development.

Self-assessment

Photocopy and complete the self-assessment chart on page 161, inserting the following topics under 'The work I have done includes':

1. Achievement of intellectual skills:
   understanding
   communication and language
2. Stimuli:
   environmental
   parental
3. Toys and activities
4. Books: selection, use and care
5. Educational provision:
   mother and baby groups
   playgroups/nursery schools
   primary schools.

Photocopy and complete the self-marking plan on page 162 for the six working briefs in this unit.

Social and Emotional Development

Core information ——————————

Social development

Socialisation

Socialisation is the process of training or adapting children to fit into the world around them. It depends upon the acquisition of **social skills** such as: consideration for others, truthfulness, honesty, good manners, self-control, obedience and independence.

To acquire these skills a child needs:

- A stable and loving background.
- To be taught the 'ground rules'.
- To be shown by example.
- Opportunities to mix with others.
- The support of family and community.
- Kind, but firm, discipline.

Pattern of social development

Age	Social development
Up to 6 months	Between six and eight weeks, the first social smile occurs. Becomes excited and pleased when a familiar figure or sound is seen or heard. Stops crying when picked up.
6 months	Friendly with strangers, beginning to show some shyness, familiar with parents and family. Explores by reaching out for adult's hair, spectacles, etc. Makes social advances to other babies and pets.
9 months	Beginning to learn feeding skills, differentiates between parent and strangers, may be suspicious of strangers. Beginning to understand the important social contact of speech.
1 year	Very sociable with known children and adults but suspicious of strangers. Shows increasing desire to be with and imitate others. Will respond to verbal commands. Is developing the social skills of feeding, dressing and potty training.
18 months	Showing signs of wanting to be independent, but is also clinging. May display assertiveness, but loves to be entertained and is quickly diverted. Can remove clothing, may have some bowel control, will imitate simple household tasks.
2 years	Demands a lot of personal attention. Personal skills are improving and good personal habits should be taught at this stage. May still be assertive and have temper tantrums if thwarted. Will watch other children play and will play near them.

$2\frac{1}{2}$ years	Carries through role play activities. Still dependent upon caring adult and does not like to be separated from parent, but realises he or she will come back if absent. Does not join in group play.
3 years	Day-time bowel and bladder control usually achieved. Ready for mixing with others at playgroup. Aware of others' needs and can show concern. Self-willed and assertive, but general behaviour more controlled. Social skills progressing, but still needs help.
4 years	Desire to play with other children, although still self-centred. Understands sharing and taking turns and has a sense of past, present and future. Becoming much more independent and will explore people and events outside the home.
5 years	From this age, the child should be a sociable, friendly individual, ready to make friends with other children and show consideration for others. May still revert to childish behaviour on occasions, but good training and discipline will give the support needed.

Family relationships

1. **Family structure** Nuclear, extended, single-parent.
   Cultural variations Ethnic, regional, religious, social class.

All these variants may increase or diminish the child's opportunities for social contact.

2. **Family roles** These used to be clearly defined but now mother and father roles are much less distinct.

A child needs a male or female adult figure upon which to model himself or herself. If the social and biological role is not clear, the child may become confused. In the majority of two-parent households, the male–female roles are still clearly and traditionally defined, especially while the children are very young. Role changes may come about from personal choice, or because of circumstances such as unemployment or illness. Traditional gender roles are strongly supported within some cultural groups. Most men help with child care and domestic tasks whether or not the mother goes out to work, but in varying degrees, and few take complete responsibility.

Caring for the children in a family is often shared between man and woman, but in many cases, especially if the woman has no outside employment or works part-time, she does most of the child caring.

3. **Position within the family – siblings** A first child, or an only child will usually have the undivided attention of the parents. This can result in the child becoming lonely, shy, selfish and unsociable, unless the parents provide opportunities for mixing with others and learning how to share and how to become independent. Brothers and sisters usually give a sense of security and belonging, and older siblings will help and encourage younger ones in social and learning skills.

Sibling rivalry will occur naturally when one child in a family feels pushed out and jealous of another. Sensible parents will:

- Avoid showing favouritism to one child.
- Avoid being over-critical of one child.
- Avoid interfering in childhood squabbles unnecessarily.
- Be fair in all things.

Each child within a family should be allowed to develop as an individual. This is especially important for twins and triplets, who are often treated as parts of a whole.

4. **Grandparents and relations** Parents should make sustained efforts to maintain close contacts with relatives.

They form part of the extended family and even if they live some distance away can be supportive and give children a feeling of belonging. Cousins can provide companionship of a similar age, while aunts and uncles make good substitute parents and are seen as familiar, comfortable figures if parents are away, or have a difficult relationship. Perhaps the most valuable of all are grandparents. They are seen as familiar, undemanding, loving receivers of confidences. They can give a child the 'spoiling' and petting which parents sometimes disapprove of or have no time for, and they can form a secure link with life outside the family circle.

Extended social relationships

Parent substitutes Opinions differ about the effects on a small child of being parted from its mother (or father). A lot depends on the child's temperament and the quality of caring received when the parents are there. In some families, economic necessity means that the mother must go back to her work soon after the birth of her child; sometimes she returns to work because she finds child rearing too isolating, restricting or tedious. Whatever the reason, it is essential to find a parent substitute who will suit the child and the parent. A good substitute could widen the child's social contacts and provide a welcome break for the parent.

Babysitters For occasional social outings, shopping, illness, etc., when a parent may need to leave a child, the choice of babysitter could be:

- Grandparents or relatives. Probably the best choice as the child will know the sitter and the parents will know they are reliable.
- Neighbours. Usually well known to the parents and therefore reliable and responsible; could do babysitting on an exchange basis.
- Babysitting club. Often arranged between groups of friends, neighbours, clinic, etc. – usually works if well organised.
- Hired babysitters. May be expensive.

Parents must check that the sitter is:

- reliable   ● experienced   ● personally recommended if possible
- introduced to the child beforehand   ● well informed about the child's needs
- sensible in an emergency   ● able to contact them or a close neighbour if necessary   ● old enough.

A regular child minder will be necessary if both parents go out to work. The choice can be:
- A private arrangement with a friend, neighbour or relative. This can be successful as the child will know the minder and the minder may be cheap and come to the child's home if the child is ill. The arrangement can fail if the minder has little experience of young children, has different methods from the parents, has other commitments or is unreliable.
- Registered child minders (often do not take babies under 1 year old). The local social services department will supply a list and friends may recommend one. Parents should check the minder's experience, attitude to and interest in children, the number of children he or she minds, the premises and facilities for outdoor play, charges, hours of opening and distance to travel.
- A creche or playgroup attached to a place of work. Very few firms have these facilities.
- Local authority day nursery. Places are limited and often priority is given to those in special need, such as children of single parents, handicapped children or those from poor home circumstances. These nurseries are quite expensive, but financial help is available for low-income families.
- Community, private or voluntary nurseries. These are organised and run by private groups or some children's charities. They often do not take children under 2 years old. Private nurseries may be expensive.

Whatever choice parents make, they should make sure that the child:

- Is well cared for, with opportunities for indoor and outdoor play.
- Is in a stimulating environment, which will encourage intellectual skills.
- Is given opportunities to mix and play with other children and adults.

Peer groups Human beings are naturally gregarious. Even babies enjoy watching other babies and cry if they are lonely; the 2-year-old plays happily alongside others, and the 3-year-old is ready for group play. Through social play, the child will learn how to make relationships, share and be cooperative. Parents should make opportunities whenever possible for their children to play with others. This can be done through: mother and baby/toddler groups; Meet-a-Mum Association; local church groups; playgroups.

Activities which involve social contact include swimming groups, visits to the zoo, play park, public library sessions, dancing and exercise classes, Cubs and Brownies.

Conditions needed for socialisation

- **Parental involvement** This includes: giving the child a secure and loving background; encouraging and giving opportunities for social mixing; teaching social skills and setting standards which will make the child acceptable to others; taking an interest in the child's progress.
- **Environment** A satisfactory environment will include places where children can socialise and play together safely. Some children live in isolated conditions such as remote farms, high rise flats, etc. In these cases parents should try to arrange situations for socialisation.
- **Toys and games which encourage sociable play**

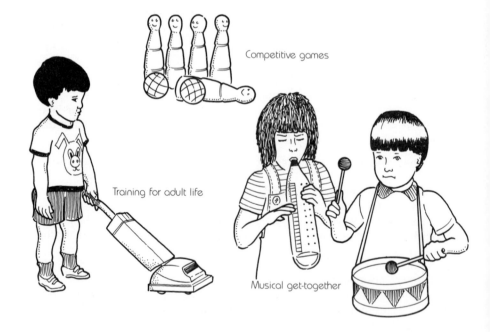

Competitive games

Training for adult life

Musical get-together

Common behaviour problems and discipline

All children at some time are badly behaved and display antisocial behaviour.

This may be due to simple physical **causes** such as:

- tiredness
- insufficient exercise
- poor diet
- sickening for an infection
- poor health,

or more complex causes such as:
- boredom   • loneliness   • over-restrictive or over-indulgent parents
- insufficient opportunities for 'letting off steam'   • lack of attention
- emotional problems causing jealousy, insecurity, frustration, etc.

The **results** of these may be: aggressive behaviour – kicking, biting or bullying other children – listlessness, constant attention seeking, quarrelling, arguing, becoming shy and uncommunicative, reverting to bed-wetting or soiling, emotional problems such as stammering, nail biting, head banging, etc.

Before these problems can be **treated**, parents must try to find the cause. Physical problems can be treated with better health care – more sleep and possibly fewer foods containing additives.

Other problems should be solved by giving the child more attention and finding out what is causing worry; for example, jealousy of a new baby, bullying from an older child, fear of starting school or going into hospital, or parents who are too demanding. The cause can then be dealt with, or, if the problem has become too deeply rooted, it may be necessary to consult the doctor, who may refer the child to a psychiatrist. Problems left untreated in childhood can lead to difficulties in making positive social relationships when the child is older.

Discipline should start when the child knows the difference between right and wrong. Undisciplined children are often over-aggressive, unmanageable and insecure. They act in an antisocial manner, which is carried through into teenage and adult life.

Discipline should be consistent, understood by the child, fair, related to the cause and quickly over. Physical punishment should be avoided. A child should never be threatened with the withdrawal of love, neither should father or a policeman be used as a disciplinary threat.
- Avoid conflict or head-on clashes if possible.
- Encourage good behaviour by giving small rewards.
- Use love-oriented methods such as giving reasons for refusal, removing the source of frustration, providing alternative pursuits, examining the child's reasons for the actions, talking and reasoning with the child, holding the child firmly and tightly and giving more attention.
- Negative methods such as slapping, long periods of isolation, shouting or ignoring often confuse and frighten a child and can lead to severe abuse by uncontrolled parents.

Emotional development

Emotional development is closely linked with the other areas of development. It may be arrested by physical or social set-backs and the child can remain babyish and immature for a long time.

Identifying emotions

Emotions are feelings. Babies and small children are unable to control their feelings and display them freely. It is easy to see which emotions are being expressed in the photographs on page 98. Some feelings are good or positive, for example, pleasure, pride, excitement, loving, caring, happiness. Some of these good feelings can be over-indulged; for example, pride can become self-destructive. Bad or negative feelings such as jealousy, anger, sorrow or shyness also vary in degree and can sometimes be directed into acceptable channels; aggression, for instance, can be **constructive** in an adult job.

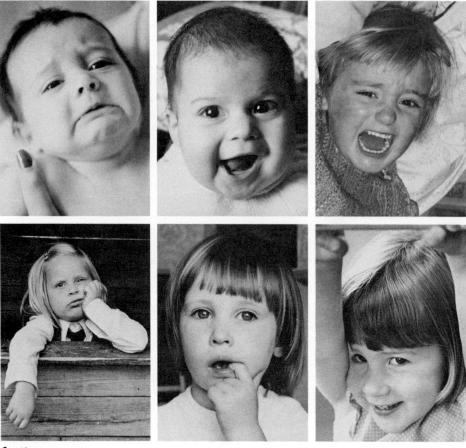

Emotions

Pattern of development

Babies feel emotions, but they are largely self-centred. They express pleasure when they are warm, well-fed, etc., and anger when uncomfortable. The **older** baby is looking beyond immediate needs and shows excitement in anticipating the arrival of food, pleasure at a familiar face, curiosity at new objects and experiences anger and frustration when thwarted.

The **1-year-old** not only responds to affection and love, but is also able to show it in kissing and hugging. The child feels insecure and worried if the carer is not in sight.

The **2-year-old** is becoming aggressive, may have a quick temper and show anger, but is also loving and easily forgets and forgives. This is quite a negative period when the child is stubborn and wilful, but also clinging to the parents.

The **3-year-old** is becoming more independent, less insecure and therefore less demanding. Ability to control emotions has developed although it is only basic. The child can become frustrated when unable to do things, but has a much more caring attitude towards people in close contact and is becoming more cooperative. As the child becomes older and more aware of people and external events, the destructive emotions of jealousy, guilt and fear will be experienced more commonly, but the child will also be better able to cope with and control them.

Emotional control

It is necessary for children to know how to handle their emotions to enable them to become acceptable members of the community. They should not be over protected and should be allowed to cope with bad and good emotional experiences, with guidance and support from carers.

Teaching emotional control requires:
- patient handling
- loving care and attention
- good examples
- satisfactory models to imitate
- careful, simple explanation and reasoning
- encouragement
- considered rewards and punishments.

The cultural background of the child is important when considering emotional development, as traditional values and expectations differ. Some ethnic communities are either less or more restrained emotionally.

Emotional problems

Causes A child is making emotional contacts from the moment of birth. If rejected, unloved and uncared for, the child will suffer emotional deprivation. This can be worse than physical neglect because the results are not immediately obvious. The child can carry emotional scars for a lifetime and pass them on to his or her own children.

Results During childhood, emotional problems may be shown as excessive fears, quarrelsomeness, bullying, destructiveness, jealousy; or nervous habits, such as nail-biting, bed-wetting, tics, stuttering, head banging; or withdrawal symptoms such as excessive shyness, clinging to mother, lying or attention seeking.

It is necessary to treat the cause, not the symptom, and to try to clear up the underlying problem. This may involve changing the parents' attitudes and adapting the family lifestyle.

Play

Well-selected toys and activities will often help the dispersal of pent-up emotions, which the child is not yet mature enough to control. Banging toys or outdoor physical activities such as jumping, climbing, etc., will release tension and aggression. Imaginative role play situations such as dressing up, or playing at mothers and fathers or doctors and nurses, will allow the child to act through worrying situations. Creative activities such as painting, modelling and collage, facilitate artistic expression and give an outward representation of feelings. In these ways the child can express feelings in positive ways, at the same time learning how to control them.

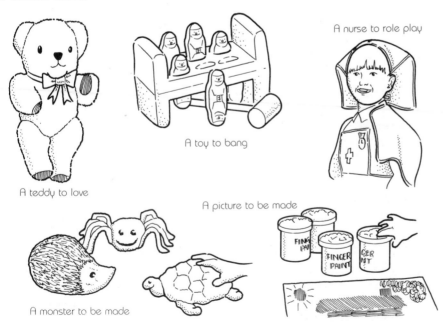

A teddy to love

A toy to bang

A nurse to role play

A picture to be made

A monster to be made

Pupil participation

Working briefs

1. Development
Individual work (Investigation)

Observe the child you are studying on several occasions, and each time fill in this checklist of the stages of social development. If you are studying a child for a period of six months or more, you can do a checklist when you start and when you finish your study and observe the progress made.

Compare the social achievements of the child you study with those of children being studied by other members of your group, in a younger or older age group. You can then accurately judge your child's level of sociability.

Stages of social development - checklist

Child's name _____ Age _____ Date _____

	Yes	No	Sometimes
Stops crying when picked up - gives a sociable smile.			
Interested in other babies, shy with strangers.			
Desires to be with others, beginning to imitate.			
Temper tantrums when thwarted, usually loving.			
Plays near other children, but not with them.			
Shows concern for others, is kind and considerate.			
General behaviour is more controlled.			
Much more independent.			
Copes with new experiences.			
Is friendly and sociable with children and adults.			
Has a best friend or best friends.			

Stage of play: Solitary _____ Parallel _____ Group _____

---

2. Social skills
Individual work (Survey)

Study a group of children, possibly at playgroup or nursery school, who are soon to start primary school. What is their standard of social skills? If possible discover some background information to help you assess which factors may help or hinder the development of social skills.

Sample observation sheet

Child	A	B	C	D	E
Age					
Girl or boy					
Single parent					
Two parents					
One parent working					
Two parents working					
Number in family					

Can the child:	Well	Fair	No
Feed himself (herself)?			
Wash his (her) hands?			
Put on shoes and fasten them?			
Put on/take off coat?			
Use a zip fastener?			
Clean his (her) teeth?			
Go to toilet unaided?			
Brush/comb hair?			
Use a handkerchief?			

Summarise your findings.

3. Parental roles

Class work (Triggers)

Study this cartoon. Discuss within your group:

What it means. What points it is trying to make.
Whether it implies that neither father nor mother are clear about their family role.

Extend your discussion to give **your** ideas about parental roles and role reversal.

4. Family relationships

Class work (Triggers)

Children love to feel part of a family. Design a simple **family tree**, like the one shown on page 102, which a 4–5-year-old could help you make. If possible use photographs in the spaces for relatives or do simple drawings.

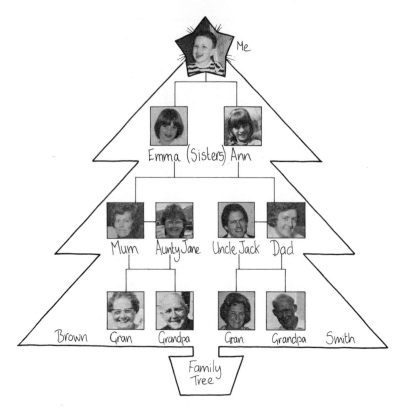

Me

Emma (Sisters) Ann

Mum   Aunty Jane   Uncle Jack   Dad

Brown   Gran   Grandpa   Gran   Grandpa   Smith

Family Tree

5. Extended social relationships   Class work (Syndicate)

Topic to investigate: the services in your area for child minding.

a) 0–3 years   b) 3–5 years   c) Part time   d) Full time.

Investigate

- The types of child minding facility which parents want.
- Which particular family situations most require a child minder.
- What is provided by the social services; LEA; private sector; voluntary sector.
- Whether there is a shortage of these services in your area.

Discover

- The different possibilities in your area.
- Where they are – draw a map.
- Which hours they are open.
- What facilities they offer; for example, meals, trained staff, garden.
- How much they charge.
- The age range they cover.
- Whether they cover school holidays as well.
- Whether parents are expected to be involved.

Make up a booklet in clear note form containing all this information. Enquire whether your local child clinic, CAB or public library would like copies.

(See example on page 108.)

6. Social and emotional problems
Group or individual work (Problem-solving)

Study the following situations; identify the possible causes of the problems; suggest courses of action which the child's parent(s) could take; and recommend people or organisations who could help.

a) Jaz is 4 years old and attends a local play group three mornings a week. His mother notices that just recently he complains of headaches and feeling sick and he seems unhappy.

b) Tracey is a single parent bringing up two young children on a limited income. The family live in a block of high-rise flats and Tracey often feels lonely and 'on edge'. The children are noisy and badly behaved and sometimes the neighbours complain.

c) Julie is nearly five and her parents are worried because she seems lonely and unhappy. She shows no affection for the new baby and seems to be returning to babyish ways since she returned home from a brief stay in hospital.

7. Play

Group activity (Collaborative learning game)

To help to develop a child's imaginative skills, and to give opportunities for social play, write a short, simple play suitable for a number of playgroup children to perform. It could be based on a well-known fairy story or it could be full of fantasy characters such as goblins, dragons, fairies or space creatures.

Make a set of masks for the play, if possible with the children helping you. Paper plates, paper bags (not plastic) and empty cereal boxes can all be converted into good masks. Children enjoy a certain amount of frightening things, but don't give them nightmares! If possible let the children perform the play.

Suggestions for masks

Written work

Fact finding exercise

1. Explain the difference between:

   Nuclear   and   extended families.
   Extrovert   and   introvert.
   Statutory   and   voluntary.

2. Explain the meaning of:

   sibling rivalry   negativism   role reversal   parent substitute.

Application of knowledge

1. State ten ways in which twins or triplets can be treated which will help them to retain their own individual personalities.

2. List ten ways in which a mother and father can become involved in their child's playgroup.

3. List ten factors you would be looking for when choosing a babysitter.

Problem solving

1. From what sources could a supply of 'dressing up' clothes and items be obtained for children's use? What safety and hygiene procedures would you follow before allowing children to use them?

2. Suggest ways in which a child can use the following things to help to develop imagination, originality and creativity:

● potato and paint ● paper of different textures and colours, such as tissue paper, newspaper, wallpaper ● pastry scraps or homemade play-dough ● old Christmas and birthday cards ● scraps of felt, buttons, cotton wool and a metal coat hanger.

Suggest how the child's work could be displayed.

Free response

1. Explain some of the ways in which grandparents can be of value to family life and how possible problems between family generations may be avoided or resolved.

2. Within a playgroup or primary class there may be children from a wide range of cultural backgrounds. Suggest ways in which the teacher or leader can use the traditions and experiences of the children and their parents to interest and stimulate them all. These could include types of dress, food, playthings and customs.

Data response

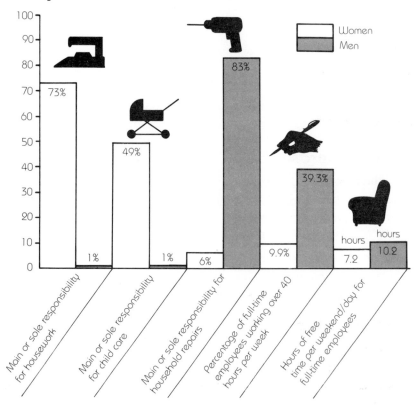

Dept of Employment/OPCS 1984, CSO 1987

This chart shows the *main* responsibilities for domestic work and child care in a family with both male and female parents. It does not indicate where tasks are shared.

1. Which group is mainly responsible for housework?

2. Which group is mainly responsible for child care?

3. Why do you think that well over three-quarters of household repairs are done by men?

4. Many mothers have full-time jobs outside the home. List some of the problems of the 'working mother', and suggest ways in which she could be helped by her partner, her employer and the state.

5. The chart indicates that, generally, male employees have more hours of free time at home than female employees. Why do you think this may be? How can parents include their children in their leisure-time activities?

Self-assessment

Photocopy and complete the self-assessment chart on page 161, inserting the following topics under 'The work I have done includes':

1. Acquisition of social skills
2. Pattern of social development
3. Interpersonal family relationships
4. Extended social relationships
5. Conditions for socialisation
6. Behaviour problems and discipline
7. Identifying emotions
8. Pattern of emotional development
9. Emotional control
10. Emotional problems
11. Play.

Photocopy and complete the self-marking plan on page 162 for the seven working briefs in this unit.

Appendices – Study area 2

Methods of presenting and recording results

Physical development (page 63)

Example 1. Safety in the home (page 79)
This is a sample quiz for parents with young children.

1. Is your home and garden safe for young children?

2. Do you have guards for all types of fire?

3. Do you keep all medicines in a locked cabinet?

4. Do you keep matches and lighters safely stored away?

5. Is your baby's cot placed away from the window?

6. Do you keep all household cleaning agents out of reach of children?

7. Do you run cold water into the baby's bath before the hot?

8. Do you keep sharp knives and garden tools out of the children's way?

9. Do you have well-lit stairs, hall and passageways?

10. Do you use a safety gate to keep small children away from dangerous places?

11. Do you check that there are no dangerous or poisonous plants in the garden?

12. Do you cover all areas of water such as garden ponds and water butts with netting?

13. Do you keep all garden gates closed and fences in good repair?

14. Do you have a basic knowledge of first aid?

Score: 14–12 very good indeed; 11–9 some improvement needed; below 9 – please take some safety measures!

Example 2. Play and toys (page 80)

Your brief is to make a toy or game for a child, with a special emphasis on safety features. A few suggestions are shown opposite.

This flow chart should help you to organise your ideas and your work:

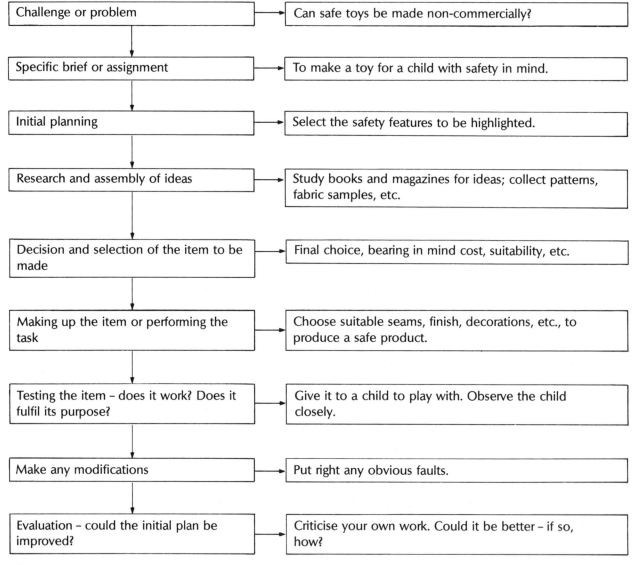

Challenge or problem → Can safe toys be made non-commercially?

Specific brief or assignment → To make a toy for a child with safety in mind.

Initial planning → Select the safety features to be highlighted.

Research and assembly of ideas → Study books and magazines for ideas; collect patterns, fabric samples, etc.

Decision and selection of the item to be made → Final choice, bearing in mind cost, suitability, etc.

Making up the item or performing the task → Choose suitable seams, finish, decorations, etc., to produce a safe product.

Testing the item – does it work? Does it fulfil its purpose? → Give it to a child to play with. Observe the child closely.

Make any modifications → Put right any obvious faults.

Evaluation – could the initial plan be improved? → Criticise your own work. Could it be better – if so, how?

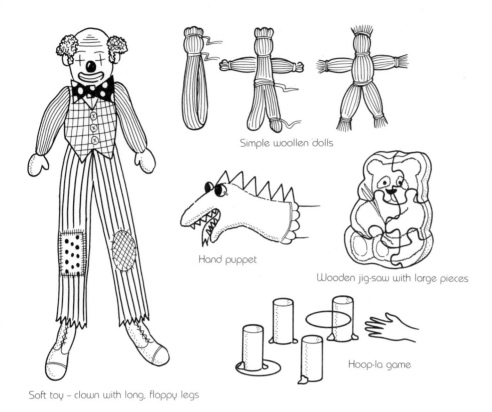

Simple woollen dolls

Hand puppet

Wooden jig-saw with large pieces

Hoop-la game

Soft toy – clown with long, floppy legs

Intellectual development (page 83)

Example 3. Speech development (page 90)

Present your information on speech development for your child study in the form of a chart. The one shown here is an example, but you could use a bar chart or a stick graph. Don't forget to summarise your conclusions. Similar facts could be charted for children in older age groups.

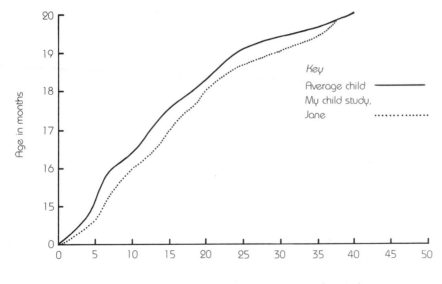

Number of words known over a six-month period

Social and emotional development (page 93)

Example 4. Child minding (page 102)

a) Design brief: to make a booklet containing information about child minding facilities in your area.

b) Planning: survey your area – decide the type of information parents need.

c) Find out the options.

d) Plan the cover and layout.

e) Plan and produce a number-coded map.

f) Make up the booklet and arrange to have several copies made.

g) Test out your product on local parents.

h) Distribute to suitable outlets, for example, child clinics and the public library.

A similar topic could be done relating to opportunities for social activities for the under-fives in your area, such as library story-telling sessions, pre-school gymnastics, etc.

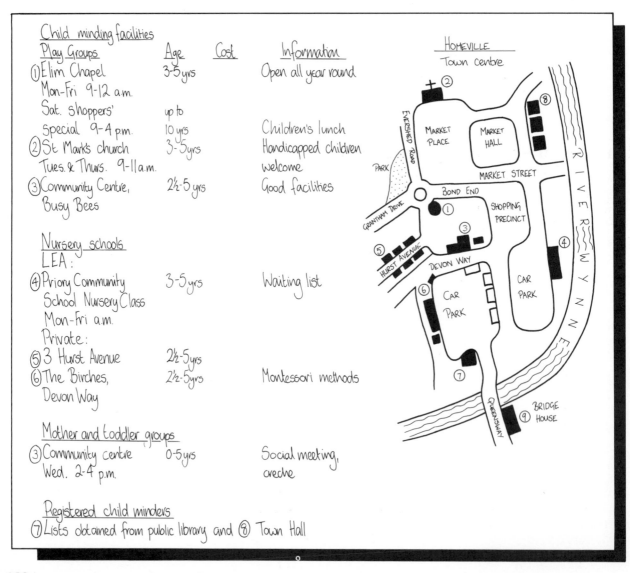

Resources guide

There is a lot of information available for this study area, so only a brief selection is given.

Physical development

Award scheme	Publisher or source
The Three Cross Award Scheme	St John's Ambulance Association

Charts and posters

'Child Development', 'The Senses'	Pictorial Charts Educational Trust
'How Diseases are Spread', safety posters	Sterling Health and RoSPA

Films

Immunisation Series, *A Lifetime of Protection*	CFL Vision
Play It Safe, Jimmy Savile	BBC video

Leaflets and booklets

Health

'Children's Teeth', 'Children's Infections'	Sterling Health
'How to Make Growing Up Child's Play'	Wyeth Nutrition
'Don't Give Your Baby a Sweet Tooth'	General Dental Council
Large selection of leaflets from Health Educational Authority (HEA)	

Safety

'Safety In Cars'	British Standards Institution
'Playing Safe with British Standards', 'Child Safety at Home'	Health Advisory Service
'Safety in the Home'	HEA
'Mind How You Go'	BBC booklet
'First Steps to Safety', 'The Home Safety Book'	Royal Society for the Prevention of Accidents (RoSPA)
First-aid manual, first-aid kits	Order of St John, Supplies Dept.

Food

A large selection of booklets and leaflets, usually free, are available from: Milupa, Wyeth Nutrition, Heinz (also available in ethnic minority languages), Milk Marketing Board, Nestlé, Robinsons, Marmite, Cow & Gate, etc.

Toys

Toy catalogues are available from: Galt, Early Learning Centre, Hamleys, Tridias, Biro, Mothercare, etc.

Intellectual development

Books	Publisher or source
Ladybird Catalogue	Ladybird Books Ltd.
Sainsbury's books for children	Sainsbury's stores
Mothercare books for children	Mothercare catalogue
Tell-a-Tale, book and cassette packs	Pickwick and Ladybird

'Teaching Your Child to Talk', etc.

'Answering a Child's Questions', 'Can't Talk Yet?'

Book Trust – publications and travelling book exhibition from the Centre for Children's Books

The College of Speech Therapists

HEA

Book Trust

Leaflets and booklets

'Coping with Kids' from BBC series *The Parent Programme*

The Humpty Dumpty Club

Macdonald 3/4/5 Nursery Course

Griffin Software Programmes

BBC Education Programmes

Odhams Leisure Group

Macdonald Educational

WH Smith, Boots, etc.

Toys

Catalogues as detailed above

The British Association for Early Childhood Education, will provide information on the welfare and education of young children (SAE needed)

Multi-ethnic rag doll pattern   Bedford

Social and emotional development

Associations   **Publisher or source**

National Childminding Association (leaflet, 'A Guide to Child Minding')

Films

He Acts his Age, The Grandmother   CFL Vision

Leaflets

'You Know More Than You Think'

'Making Playgrounds', Planning and Building teaching pack

'Child's Craft', teaching pack

'Twins in the Family'

HEA and MIND

Community Service Volunteers

Knitting Craft Group

Robinsons Baby Foods

Magazines

Practical Parenting, Practical Health

Under Five

Family Circle Publications

Pre-school Playgroups Association

Family and Community

UNIT ONE

Family life

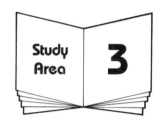

Study
Area | 3

Core information

Family

Family structures

There are many types of modern family group. The traditional 'typical' family group of married couple with two dependent children and father only in employment represents only one in twenty households.

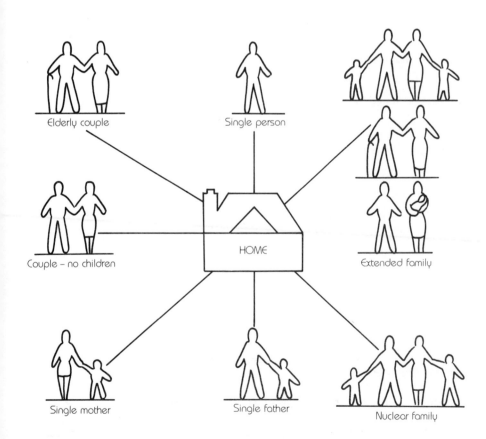

Elderly couple

Single person

Couple – no children

HOME

Extended family

Single mother

Single father

Nuclear family

Family groups

People by type of household

Great Britain	Percentage
Couple with dependent children	45
Couple with no children or with non-dependent children	32
Lone parent with dependent or non-dependent children	9
One person only	10
Other	4

General Household Survey 1985 (OPCS)

As this chart shows: 45 per cent of households consist of couples with dependent children.
9 per cent of households are lone parents with children.

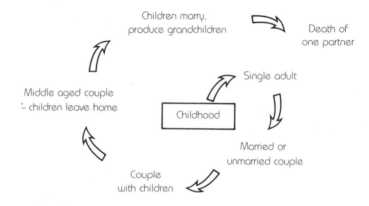

Typical simple lifecycle

The illustration here shows a typical simple life cycle. It may be complicated or interrupted by:
● separation ● divorce ● widowhood/widowerhood ● lone parenthood
● remarriage ● step-families.

It is widely accepted that children thrive well and feel secure if they have all or some of the following conditions:
● two parents – usually married ● a settled home background ● family relatives and friends ● siblings ● parents who share the responsibilities of child rearing ● uncomplicated family relationships.

Functions

The family unit is there to:
● **Provide** a secure, caring base for children to grow up in.
● **Care for** the needs of its weaker members, for example, those who are sick, handicapped or elderly.
● **Support** all its members, encouraging children to leave home at the right time and return when they wish.
● **Encourage** socialisation, extending beyond the family and into the community.
● **Teach** cultural traditions and values.

The UK is a multi-racial, multi-cultural and multi-religious society, made up from many ethnic groups. Each culture tries to preserve its traditions and background, bringing a wealth of cultural diversity to our society.

Ethnic groups	% of population	
White	95%	mainly UK born
Indian	1%	30–40% UK born
Pakistani/Bangladeshi	1%	
West Indian	1%	50% UK born
Others – Chinese, African, etc	2%	

General Household Survey 1985

The children in the picture are preserving their cultural heritage in costume, song and dance.

Children should be brought up to be proud of their cultural background and taught to accept that children of other cultures may have different, but equally valuable, traditions of dress, food, music, religion and family life. The community must make provisions for the varying beliefs of ethnic groups; for example, within Asian families it is more acceptable for females to help at a birth and there is a preference for female medical staff to be in attendance during pregnancy.

Social change

Changing social attitudes towards issues such as illegitimacy, cohabitation, divorce and gender roles within the family have brought about radical reforms in family life. Some of these changes are good, in that old taboos and moral double standards are being altered, but often the victims of some of the negative aspects of these changes have been the children in the family.

Facts:
Illegitimacy 21.4 per cent of all live births in 1986 were illegitimate, although two thirds were registered by both parents (indicating a stable relationship). This compares with a 19.2 per cent illegitimacy rate in 1985.

Premarital cohabitation A much higher percentage of couples are living together before marriage. In 1985, 5 per cent of all women aged 18–49 were living with men to whom they were not married.

Marriage In 1986, there were 347 924 marriages in England and Wales, only 63 per cent being between bachelors and spinsters. First-time marriages have been falling and there is a rise in remarriage.

Teenage marriages are quite rare – in 1986 only 3 per cent of bridegrooms and 10 per cent of brides were under 20 years old (1971 – 9 per cent and 27 per cent). In 1986, the average age for first marriage was 26.3 years (men) and 24.1 years (women). Two thirds of all new marriages are still more likely to end with the death of a partner rather than with divorce.

Divorce In 1986, there was a total of 154 000 divorces in England and Wales, a 4 per cent fall compared with 1985 (160 000). However, the increase in 1985 was 11 per cent up on the previous year and the general trend is upwards.

In 1986, 5000 couples divorced after one year
9000 couples divorced after two years.

One-parent families Failing marriage leaves many children in a single-parent family or step-family and, in 1986, 163 000 children were affected by divorce. However, not all one-parent families are a result of divorce or separation.

One in eight children in Britain lives in a one-parent family.

Nine out of ten lone parents are women.

Two thirds of lone mothers are divorced or separated. The National Council for One-Parent Families (NCOPF) estimates that about one million one-parent families in Britain are caring for over 1.6 million children. Although many single parents manage to provide a happy, stable home for their children, they often have to cope with problems such as:

- low income   - loneliness   - poor housing   - critical social attitudes
- few opportunities for leisure activities   - stress and worry.

Children living in such situations may:

- be stressed   - develop emotional problems   - suffer isolation
- be abused   - be undernourished   - feel insecure and different from
other children   - be neglected.

Family finance

The UK is regarded as a prosperous member of the EEC, with its inhabitants enjoying a high standard of living, especially when compared to that of some developing countries. However, everyone in the UK does not enjoy the same living standards and there is a large gap between rich and poor, usually most obvious between:

- employed and unemployed   - single- and two-parent households
- large and small families   - different age groups   - different areas of
the country   - social classes.

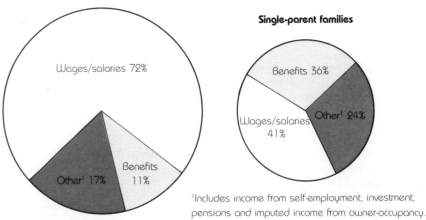

All families with children

Wages/salaries 72%

Other[1] 17%   Benefits 11%

Single-parent families

Benefits 36%

Wages/salaries 41%   Other[1] 24%

[1]Includes income from self-employment, investment, pensions and imputed income from owner-occupancy.

Sources of income   Family Expenditure Survey 1985

Income is usually 'earned income' from the wages of one or both parents; some income comes from investments or pensions and some from state benefits. Note the differences between two-parent and single-parent families. In 1984, the **average** household income for the top 20 per cent was £19 750 per year; for the bottom 40 per cent it was £2535 per year. The average for all households was £8130 per year.

In 1957 the average weekly wage was £12.50 per week.
In 1987 the average weekly wage was £190 per week: £203 for men, £134 for women

(Family Expenditure Survey 1985)

Consumer goods have risen in price over this period, but nevertheless wages have risen faster.

The pie chart shows how families in 1987 spent their income.

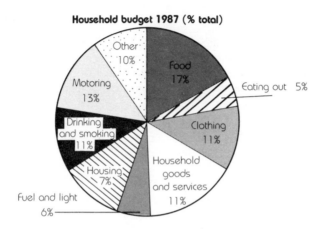

Household budget 1987 (% total)

The bar chart shows how ownership of 'luxury' items and house ownership increased in a 30-year period. Increasing prosperity means that 16 million people took trips abroad in 1987 compared with 2 million in 1957; 85 per cent of households have a telephone; there is a much higher percentage of alcohol consumed; and there are other features indicating prosperity.

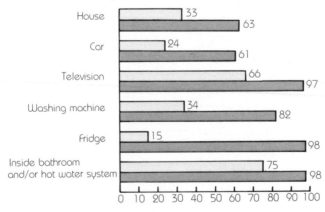

% of households owning a:

% of average household expenditure on:

Which? 1987

Although these figures give an impression of increasing prosperity, there are still large numbers of families living in poverty. In 1986 202 000 families were in receipt of family income supplement (FIS)* (42% were one-parent families).

3 880 000 children were in low income families.
2 030 000 children were in low income families on or below supplementary benefit level*.
Local authorities in England accepted over 100 000 households as homeless.
1 269 000 children were in families with an unemployed main earner. (Shelter, FPSC)
Although owner-occupied housing has increased, 20 000 properties were repossessed in 1986 due to mortgage arrears.

Unemployment is one of the major factors which contributes to low income. Although unemployment is falling – from 3.1 million (February 1987) to 2.5 million (February 1988) this still leaves a large number of families who are dependent on state benefits. Income Support provides a family of two unemployed adults and two children under 11 with £72.95 a week (April 1988).

It is especially important that financial budgeting is considered in low-income families. It is estimated (Family Policy Studies Centre Report 1987) that 51 per cent of single-parent families cut down their food intake because of shortage of money. The National Child Development Study concludes that poor school performance in some children from lone-parent families is because of low income rather than lone parenthood.

Family spending

Spending patterns vary with the type of household involved. The chart shows how household income in 1985 was spent on the three essentials, housing, fuel and food, according to household type. In the lower income groups, almost 60 per cent is spent on these essentials, leaving only 40 per cent for clothing, transport, leisure, etc.

Household spending patterns

Type of household	Percentages		
	Housing	*Fuel*	*Food*
Low income pensioner	13	17	31
Single parent with two or more children	12	9	26
Man and woman with two children	16	6	22
Man and woman with four or more children	13	7	24
Income level			
Bottom fifth	14	13	29
Top fifth	15	4	17
All UK households	16	6	20

Employment Gazette December 1986

*FIS and supplementary benefit were replaced with family credit and income support in April 1988.

The spending of money within a household usually works on one of four systems.

1. Whole wage system. One partner (usually the woman) manages all household finance (14%).

2. Allowance system. The man (usually) gives his partner a set amount of housekeeping money (22%).

3. Pooling system. Both partners are responsible for shared income and expenditure (56%).

4. Independent management system. Both partners manage their own money (9%).

The Pahl Study (1982–3) shows the proportion of couples in each category. These are the figures shown in brackets after each system. Obviously the pooling system is most popular, especially when the wife is earning. The New Earnings Survey (1987) suggests that on average a woman's earnings are lower than those of a man.

Housing

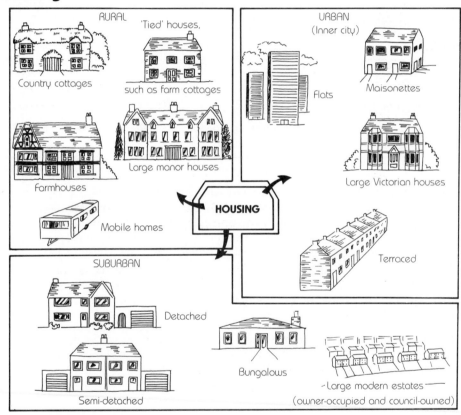

Types of housing

There is a vast selection of accommodation available at different prices. Couples just setting up home may have to take what is available at the price they can afford. Housing requirements have changed greatly over the past 150 years. The big Victorian houses required for large numbers of children and extended families have been replaced by smaller houses on modern housing estates.

    In 1890, 10% of households owned their own home.
    In 1956, 33% of households owned their own home.
    In 1986, 63% of households owned their own home.

Points to consider are:
- Rented property may be privately owned or council owned, and it is often difficult to obtain.

- Private housing is expensive to buy and needs constant upkeep. First-time buyers can often get a 100 per cent mortgage, but keeping up payments can cause problems. 'Housing Debtline' has been set up to give advice with mortgage repayment problems.
- The cost of housing varies considerably in different parts of the country. A house in London can cost more than three times as much as a similar house in parts of the north.
- Starting family life with in-laws can lead to friction.
- Over three quarters of the population live in urban areas, mainly in large towns such as London, Birmingham or Glasgow.
- Although many families live on the outskirts of towns, only about 13 million people live in rural areas.
- Urban decay in the large inner cities causes many problems and can encourage vandalism and crime.

Some families or individuals find themselves homeless because:

- they cannot make the rent or mortgage repayments   - they have to move out of a tied house   - a private landlord requires the accommodation
- they are suffering marital breakdown   - they are teenagers who have moved out of their family home with no other accommodation.

Homelessness

	1981	1983	1985
Number of families homeless	81 000	89 000	109 000
Number of homeless families with one or more dependent children	53 000	55 000	68 000

Social Trends 1987

In the first half of 1987, 53 500 households were accepted as homeless, twice the level of 1978. The housing organisation Shelter estimates that more than 80 000 young people are made homeless in any one year. The Housing (Homeless Persons) Act (1977 and 1985) makes it a statutory duty for local councils to provide accommodation for unintentionally homeless persons. These include:

- families with children under 16   - pregnant women   - those homeless because of emergency, such as fire   - those who are disabled, seriously ill or handicapped   - people of retirement age   - battered women
- young people at risk

Homeless persons should go to the homeless persons section of the local housing department. They can also get advice from the CAB. The council may put homeless persons into temporary accommodation such as:

- a council hostel   - short-life council-owned property   - bed and breakfast accommodation.

Homeless families (England). Comparison of last quarter of 1984 and 1985

	1984	1985	Percentage increase
	(thousands)		
Homeless households accepted	20.4	23.6	16
Households in temporary accommodation	11.8	14.2	20
Households in bed and breakfast	3.3	4.3	30
Households in hostels	4.0	4.6	14
Households in short-life housing	4.5	5.4	20

Department of the Environment

The number of homeless households in bed and breakfast accommodation has increased by as much as 250 per cent between 1984 and 1987. Accommodation tends to be overcrowded and of a low standard and leads to problems of:

- malnutrition
- poor hygiene
- high accident and infection risks
- behaviour disorders
- poor opportunities for social and physical development.

Although these types of accommodation are supposed to be temporary, many families have to wait years for permanent housing. Poor housing and environmental conditions can seriously damage all aspects of a child's development and cause stress in the family and marital breakdown.

Consumer buying

No-one wants to waste money and all buyers want reliability at a fair price for small or large items. The responsibility for achieving this lies with the buyer.

Before making a purchase, seek out **advice** and **guidance**, especially for large items such as prams or cots and consumables such as nappies and baby foods, which can cost a lot of money.

- Look through magazines such as *Good Housekeeping, Which?* and parenting magazines, as well as catalogues, to compare prices and value.
- Watch and listen to consumer programmes on TV and radio.
- Survey shops and get the advice of sales assistants; seek out discount stores and factory shops.
- Ask friends, neighbours, relations and the health visitor at the clinic.
- Study the labels on various products, to find out which offers best value for money.
- Look for labels such as these, which indicate safety and reliability.
- Use the CAB or Consumer Advice Centres. Send for leaflets from the British Standards Institute. The BSI sets standards, tests and awards a safety mark to show that a product has been tested for safety. It also awards a kitemark which shows that the BSI has checked the manufacturer's claim that the product meets the accepted standards of safety and quality.

Kitemark

BEAB Mark

The buyer should assess:

- safety
- design
- durability
- ease of use
- ease of cleaning
- aesthetic appeal
- guarantees and servicing.

Avoid impulse buying just because an item looks nice or is cheap. For expensive items, it is possible to buy on **credit**, but remember:

BSI Safety mark

- Some credit methods are cheaper than others. Credit terms almost always involve paying interest.
- Excessive credit can cause financial problems.
- The original trader can often claim back the goods if payments are not kept up.

Methods of credit buying include:

Banks Overdrafts, personal loans, credit cards (for example, Visa and Access).
Stores Own credit card systems (for example, at Mothercare and Debenhams), extended terms, hire purchase terms.
Mail order Catalogue buying: payments spread over several months.

Here are some ideas for obtaining goods cheaply:

- Reduced prices in shops – on items that are slightly damaged, shop-soiled, end of range or special offers.
- 'Seconds' from market stalls or factory shops.

- Secondhand goods from friends, newspaper adverts, adverts in shop windows or the clinic.
- Jumble sales, car boot sales or auctions.
- Exchanges with friends or relations.

'Bargains' obtained in these ways are not bargains if they:

- do not work
- are unsafe
- do not fit
- are badly damaged
- are past the sell-by date
- are unhygienic.

Most items obtained in these ways cannot be returned, carry no guarantee and are not covered by consumer laws. The law can provide **consumer protection**, that is, protect the buyer from unscrupulous traders and also protect traders from customers who default. When something is purchased, the trader enters into a contract with the buyer and anything sold must be:

- of merchantable quality
- fit for its purpose
- as described.

If goods do not fulfil these requirements, the contract has been broken and the buyer can make a claim.

Customers who wish to complain about faulty goods or services should follow this procedure: Complain to the trader, shop manager or private seller. If the goods are under guarantee, complain also to the manufacturer. Seek advice from the CAB or local Trading Standards Department. The Environmental Health Department deals with environmental complaints. Take the trader to court using the small claims procedure. If legal advice is needed, consult a solicitor. Legal aid may be available.

Community

The social services

Most countries have some form of social welfare which includes programmes catering for old age, invalidity and death, sickness and maternity, work injury, family allowances and housing. In 1987, the UK spent £44 billion on social security. This money is obtained from taxes and National Insurance (NI) contributions. Most people between 16 and pensionable age have to pay NI. Every school leaver receives an NI number card with a personal number printed on it. Contributions will then be assessed according to the type of earnings. The unemployed require their NI number to claim benefits. The social security system received a major overhaul in 1987–8 when the **Social Security Act** came into force, based on reforms recommended by the Secretary of State for Social Security. The aims of this Act are to:

- simplify and modernise the system
- give help where it is most needed
- streamline the system, making it more efficient
- improve help available for the disabled and long-term sick
- overhaul unemployment and housing benefits and review the 'poverty trap'.

In practice, some people are better off and some are worse. Information about benefits can be obtained from:

- local post office
- health visitor
- local DSS office
- social services department of the local council
- DSS Freephone
- leaflets/booklets issued by the DSS.

Benefits available include free prescriptions, free milk and vitamins, NHS dental treatment, help with cost of glasses and travel to hospital. The local council Social Services departments may provide: home helps, meals on wheels, home adaptations, laundry services, TV and radio, free recreational and sports facilities and outings, telephones, day centres and residential care, rehabilitation, job training and employment for the handicapped, unemployed and for offenders, parking and travel concessions, and help and advice from social workers.

The National Health Service

The NHS came into existence in 1948, introduced by Aneurin Bevan, then Minister of Health.

The basic aims were:

- To make services free and meet costs from general taxation.
- To ensure efficiency in planning and running of services and hospitals.
- To allow freedom of choice for patients and doctors, dentists and health workers.

The system is run by the Department of Health and operates at three levels, regional, area and district.

The NHS is very popular and has helped to achieve free medical care for all. Standards of health have improved, infant mortality rates have dropped and life expectancy has increased as a result of the NHS. It is, however, very expensive to run. In 1986, the UK spent £22 400 million, or £400 per person, on health care. This money is provided from general taxation. The average family paid £1600 per year in taxes for the NHS in 1986 (£570 a year in 1979). Criticisms of the NHS include poor forward planning, inadequate staffing in some areas, over-staffing in others, and long waiting lists for operations and treatment. An overhaul of the system is anticipated, with an emphasis on preventive medicine and private health schemes. The NHS provides:

- A primary health care team, usually based on a local health centre. This team deals with: general health care in the practice; ambulance and domiciliary care; emergency care; medico–social care; preventive measures; health education.
- Maternity and child care, including family planning.
- Specialist treatments such as heart, lung or joint replacements and treatments for infertility.
- Services for elderly people, including residential and day care.
- Hospital treatment, long-term or day care and treatment for outpatients.
- Research.

Emphasis is being placed on community caring and every effort is made to keep the handicapped and elderly in their own homes, giving support services to them and their families or carers.

Preventive measures are very important and cover a wide span. Such measures include:

- immunisation ● genetic counselling ● breast and cervical checks
- amniocentesis and scans ● hearing, sight and dental checks
- health education on topics such as sexually transmitted diseases (STDs), including AIDS ● accident prevention education ● school medical checks
- health and fitness campaigns which discourage alcohol and drug abuse and consumption of tobacco and encourage exercise and healthy eating.

These preventive measures plus efficient medical care, well-run hospitals and technological advances should result in less disease and better health.

Voluntary organisations

Voluntary work plays a large part in the running of the social and health services. The professional, paid workers in these services are supported and helped by well-run charities, organisations and individuals. Volunteers help the disadvantaged in the community and in doing so can be part of a caring service.

Voluntary work can be done by people:

- in any age group ● using a wide range of skills ● in any social class
- for short or long periods of time ● at any educational level ● who have a handicap.

There are three main types of voluntary work:

- Individuals who work for a hospital, help with a club for the elderly or handicapped, read to the blind, do hospital or prison visiting, etc.
- Groups of volunteers who give specific aid, for example, the Women's Royal Voluntary Service (WRVS), Relate (previously Marriage Guidance), CAB, Samaritans and Alcoholics Anonymous.
- Staff, money raisers and helpers in the thousands of charity organisations which exist, for example, Oxfam and Age Concern.

There are Volunteer Bureaux in most large towns, which coordinate volunteer workers and the people who need them. The National Council for Voluntary Organisations helps to coordinate nationally the work of voluntary organisations.

Pupil participation

Working briefs

1. Family structures

Class work (Survey)

Great Britain	Percentages		
	1976	1981	1985
1 adult	6	7	8
2 adults	13	13	15
Youngest person 0–4	15	13	13
Youngest person 5–15	22	22	18
3 or more adults	11	13	12
2 adults (1 or both over 60)	17	17	17
1 adult 60+	15	15	16

General Household Survey 1985 (OPCS)

The table above shows the percentage of households with varying family types. Survey the same information in the families of members of your group. Extend your survey to include a group in another year in your school. Express your results as a bar chart and compare them with the table above – do the percentages differ much?

2. Family functions

Class work (Triggers)

The table on page 123 is the result of a survey carried out on a housing estate in Bristol. It gives an indication of how and where families under stress with young children get help and advice. Analyse the information, pinpointing the most popular sources of help and the least popular.

Within your group discuss:

a) Why more parents seek advice from a health visitor than neighbours.
b) Where each member of your group would seek help, and why.
c) The types of problem parents are likely to require help with.
d) Other sources of help you could suggest.

Where help is sought with worries	Yes
Own family	57%
Parents	60%
Other relatives	40%
Friends	44%
Neighbours	18%
Health visitor	74%
Social worker	21%
Doctor (GP)	60%
Family Centre	8%
Home care assistant	3%
Teacher	21%
Day nursery staff	9%
Nursery school staff	13%
Psychologist	3%
Tenants' Association	5%
Midwife	14%
Other	2%

3. Social change   Group and class work (Debate)

The results of a survey of 3000 people by Social and Community Planning
Research (*British Social Attitudes* 1987) showed that:

Working
women
{
75 per cent think that the mother of a child under five
should not work at all.
17 per cent think that she should only work part time.

Family
finance
{
61 per cent think that family finance should be managed by
each partner taking from a common pool.
33 per cent think that family finance should be managed by
an allowance system – one partner manages the money
giving the other an allowance.
5 per cent think each partner should have independent
finance.

Divorce
{
40 per cent think that divorce should be made more
difficult.
25 per cent think that divorce should not be made more
difficult.

Government
spending
{
50 per cent think that more money should be spent on the
National Health Service.
25 per cent think that education should have top priority.

These are four important issues. Divide into groups to debate each one. Appoint a
group leader to report the results of the debate to the rest of the class.

4. Housing   Individual and class work (Triggers/Guest speakers)

Problem solving:

1. Sarah and her two children were made homeless when she was abandoned by her partner. The council housed her in temporary bed and breakfast accommodation, but she finds the place dirty, unhygienic and dangerous for children. It is overcrowded, with shared toilets and bathrooms, and there is nowhere for the children to play. She and the children are undernourished and have a lot of illness and the children are becoming badly behaved and unruly.

2. Parveen has arrived in England with her family and been housed in a tower block of flats. She understands little English, knows no one and has little understanding of the community she lives in. Her husband is out working all day and does not give her much money. The family are sometimes harassed by groups of youths. Parveen feels that her children are becoming unhappy and she feels lonely and depressed.

3. Kevin's wife has walked out on him, leaving him to look after their two children. He cannot now afford the high mortgage repayments on the house which they were both buying. The building society has threatened to repossess the house. Kevin has had to give up work to look after the children.

Get together some information relating to these problems. Invite a speaker from your local council housing department or Shelter, or a person in charge of your local Asian Centre, to talk to your group about housing options. Then decide:

• How these three families could help themselves to have a better life.
• What help is available from the community to assist in these situations.

5. Consumer buying   Individual work
(Collaborative learning game)

1. Child's shoe – sole comes away after two weeks' wear

2. Can of baby food with fly in it

3. Doll's head comes off, sharp prong revealed

4. Child's dress shrinks 2 cm after first wash

5. Apples sold as 1 lb weigh only ¾ lb

6. Teat parts from top of baby's dummy after only two or three uses

7. Dried milk formula sold after sell by date

Problems associated with baby/child consumer goods

Which course of action from the following list would be most suitable for each of the situations shown in the seven illustrations?

a) Look for the kitemark.
b) Go to the CAB or Consumer Advice Centre.
c) Take the item back to the shop.
d) Go to the Environmental Health Department.
e) Consult the police.
f) Take the item to the Trading Standards Department.
g) Write to the manufacturer.

Develop this into a card-matching learning game by drawing and colouring copies of action cards, like these illustrations. Make up more examples of your own.

6. Social services
Individual work (Poster)

The chart shows that quite a large percentage of people who are entitled to benefits do not take them up for reasons which include being too proud to 'accept charity', not knowing that they are eligible and not knowing how to claim. Note that in April 1988 state benefits changed; family credit replaced family income supplement.

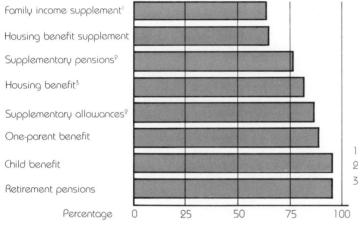

1. Combined 1983 and 1984 data
2. Figures are for 1983
3. Certificate *plus* standard housing benefit combined.

Social Trends 1988

Take-up of selected social security benefits, 1984

Produce posters which explain clearly how and what to claim, who is eligible and where to go to claim benefits for: single parents; low-income families; the sick and handicapped; the unemployed; those with housing problems; the elderly.

(See example on page 152.)

7. Voluntary work
Individual or class community work

Voluntary work can take many forms and charities are always in need of money. The United Nations Children's Fund organised a competition for young writers of children's stories to produce a bed-time story for Prince Harry. The best ones were published as a book, and the competitors were asked to find a sponsor for each line they wrote.

Copy this idea. Everyone in your group could write a short story for children, finding sponsors for each line. The best stories could be collected together in a book and the money raised could be sent to a children's charity.

Think of other money-raising schemes which could help you with your work and also help children in need.

Written work

Fact finding

1. Write an account of the work of each of the following:
   Gingerbread   Shelter   Consumer Advice Centres   British Standards
   Institute.

2. Find out about and write a paragraph on:
   a) The history of community health care.
   b) State benefits for families in EEC countries.
   c) Contrasts in child rearing in countries such as the USA, the UK, Bangladesh
      and the Chinese Republic.
   d) Helping children through the trauma of divorce.

Application of knowledge

1. Explain the terms:
   indigenous population   poverty trap   mortgage default
   short-life housing   reconstituted families.

2. Describe the work done by:

   a psychiatric social worker   a community nurse
   an obstetrician   a health education officer.

3. Write out a set of at least ten rules for family shopping. For example, 'Try to
   leave the children behind when making important purchases', 'Don't be
   persuaded or intimidated by the shop assistant', 'Avoid impulse buys', etc.

Free response

One local authority is providing a nappy changing room in a male public
convenience at a cost of £25 000. Suggest possible reasons for this and discuss the
needs of the lone father in today's society.

Data response

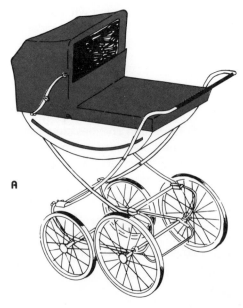

A

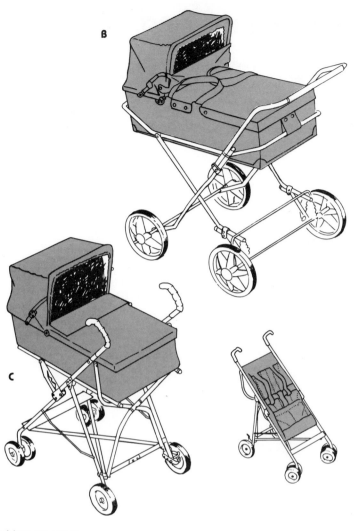

Types of child transporters

	Marks
1. Name and briefly describe the three types of child transporter shown above.	3
2. Compare the efficiency of the three types when in use.	3
3. a) Suggest an approximate cost for each transporter. b) Give **three** methods of purchasing the article on credit.	3
4. a) When buying a secondhand pram of the type shown in picture A, what points would you look for? How would you clean it ready for use?	5
b) Are secondhand goods covered by the same consumer laws as new goods?	1

5. How can a child's physical wellbeing and intellectual development be stimulated and improved by:
   a) Putting a young baby in his or her pram out in the garden?
   b) Taking a 12-month-old child to the park in his or her pushchair?
	10

	25

Self-assessment and marking

Photocopy and complete the self-assessment chart on page 161, inserting the following topics under 'The work I have done includes':

Family:
1. Structures
2. Functions
3. Social change
4. Family finance
5. Housing
6. Consumer buying

Community:
1. Social services
2. National Health Service
3. Voluntary organisations.

Photocopy and complete the self-marking plan on page 162 for the seven working briefs in this unit.

Handicaps

Core information

Some children are unable to develop normally because of **medical**, **social** or **economic** factors, which may be independent or interrelated.

Physical and mental handicaps

A handicap is anything which prevents a person from achieving full potential. Improved antenatal care and screening and genetic counselling have reduced the numbers of handicapped babies being born, but many handicapped babies who would previously have died now survive because of improved medical technology.

In every thousand babies born:

- 40–50 have some abnormality or defect.   ● 30–40 need some kind of extra care.   ● 12 have a serious handicap.   ● 4 require life-saving surgery.
- 4 are severely mentally handicapped.

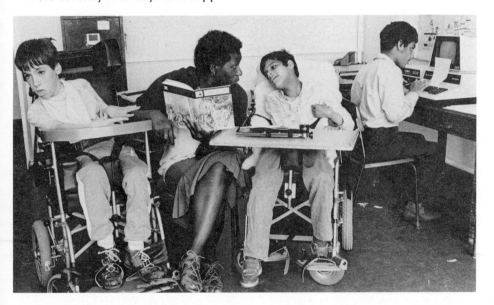

A handicapping condition can be:

Physical
- Minor conditions such as extra toes or birthmarks.
- Serious conditions such as spina bifida or club foot.
- Chronic conditions such as asthma or epilepsy.

Sensory
- Affecting vision, hearing or speech.

Mental
- Handicaps such as Down's Syndrome or brain damage.
- Mental retardation in a mild or severe form.

Emotional
- Resulting in physical or mental conditions.

The resulting handicap can be any one, or any combination, of these conditions.

Causes of handicaps

Prenatal conditions

- Maternal infections during pregnancy, for example, German measles and other viral infections which affect the developing foetus and may cause disabling conditions.
- Genetic abnormalities, that is, conditions which are passed on through the family. Cystic fibrosis, sickle-cell anaemia, colour blindness and haemophilia are examples of conditions caused by abnormal genes.
- Inadequate care during pregnancy; for example, women who smoke or take drugs or alcohol during pregnancy put their unborn babies at risk.
- Exposure to radiation and environmental pollution, for example, excess lead can harm the foetus.
- Poor diet, lack of rest and excessive exercise can produce a malnourished baby.
- Sexual infections such as syphilis or AIDS can infect the foetus.

Many defective foetuses are naturally aborted before birth.

Conditions at birth

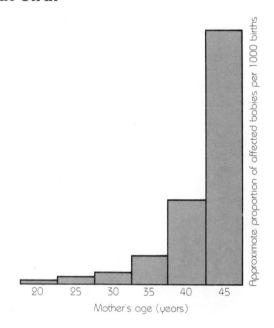

Down's syndrome

- Congenital malformation (those present at birth). In the 1 in 20 babies born with malformations, many defects are only minor or easily corrected. More serious defects include: double ureter, male hernia, spina bifida, hydrocephalus, cleft palate and Down's Syndrome. Causes are not always known but include genetic factors, parents' age, geographical location and the social environment.
- Pre-term or low birthweight babies may be at risk and may require care in a special care unit. One in seven new born babies need this.
- A complicated birth may result in the baby being starved of oxygen, resulting in brain damage.

Postnatal conditions

- Despite routine tests before and after birth, many abnormal conditions cannot be detected until the baby grows. This is why regular checks are important.

- Childhood illnesses and infections, such as whooping cough, mumps and rheumatic fever, can leave permanent damage.
- Poor diet and poor environmental conditions can increase the risk of infection, cause malnutrition, obesity and disease, which in turn can result in life-long damage.
- Accidental and non-accidental injury. Large numbers of children are left permanently handicapped from accidents in the home, the environment and on the roads. Non-accidental injury (child abuse) affects possibly one in ten children, causing physical and emotional damage (see pages 142–4).
- Physical neglect and lack of stimulation, for example, not being spoken to or played with, can retard a child's development.

Diagnosis, prevention and treatment

Early and accurate diagnosis of abnormal conditions means that many can be prevented from developing or given early treatment.

Condition – diagnosis	Preventive measures	Treatment
Prenatal Chromosomal conditions (such as Down's syndrome, sickle-cell anaemia) and inherited risk conditions (such as cystic fibrosis, haemophilia) can be diagnosed during the first 8–12 weeks of pregnancy, or may be suspected if previously seen in the family.	Chorion villi sampling, (CVS) test given up to twelfth week of pregnancy, will detect many abnormal conditions.	Genetic counselling; early abortion can be offered (only up to 28th week).
Viral infection risks, over exposure to X-rays and drugs, can be detected at 8–17 weeks. Spina bifida, brain abnormalities, severe heart and kidney defects and limb disorders can be detected at 25–8 weeks.	Ultra-sound scan at 16–17 weeks to check foetal development, amniocentesis test at 16 weeks to screen for spina bifida, etc.	Pregnant woman will be given necessary bed rest, medication, special diet, intra-uterine transfusion.
Rhesus incompatibility, anaemia, pre-eclampsia and high blood pressure during pregnancy can all affect the health of the foetus.	Blood tests and alphafoeto protein (AFP) tests to detect brain and spinal cord defects.	
Risk of physical/mental handicap because of mothers being addicted to alcohol or drugs, infected with an STD or smoking excessively, poor diet; environmental factors.	Urine and blood tests. Use of foetoscope to look for abnormalities. Health education for children at school and for adults by books, magazines, TV, etc. Sufficient financial help during pregnancy; provision of good antenatal care.	Counselling, vitamin and mineral supplements, medical advice.
At birth Congenital malformation – minor ones include extra fingers, birthmarks; more serious are club foot, clicky hip, Down's syndrome, hydrocephalus. An undeveloped foetus may have incomplete organs. Lack of oxygen at birth can cause mild to severe brain damage.	Genetic research resources for medical research, good antenatal care; early diagnosis by using tests which check hips, mouth, heart, abdomen and automatic reflexes.	Immediate life saving operation may be needed; care in special baby unit; special diets; parent counselling.

Condition – diagnosis	Preventive measures	Treatment
Postnatal Conditions which are not obvious at birth include: hearing and sight impairment; speech and feeding problems, such as coeliac disease; and slow physical and mental development. They must be diagnosed later at the child health clinic.	Regular developmental testing, sight and hearing tests and mobility tests are all carried out by the health visitor or clinic nurse. On the sixth day, Guthrie test for phenylketonuria (PKU).	Health visitor may suggest ways of helping with impaired mental development. Special diets and physiotherapy may be needed.
Infectious diseases and common illnesses can leave permanent damage such as ear infections, sight impairment and chest and heart weaknesses.	Infectious diseases can be prevented or made less serious if the child is protected by immunisation. A vaccine is given which provides the necessary antibodies.	Treatment is usually with bed rest and home nursing. Antibiotics only help with secondary infections.
Accidental and non-accidental injury, such as burns, scars, internal injuries, broken bones, etc. can cause emotional scars which never heal.	Safety education, first-aid courses; educating young people for parenthood; social support for families with problems.	

Care for the handicapped child

Health care teams, which care for handicapped children and their families, divide into primary health care and specialist health care.

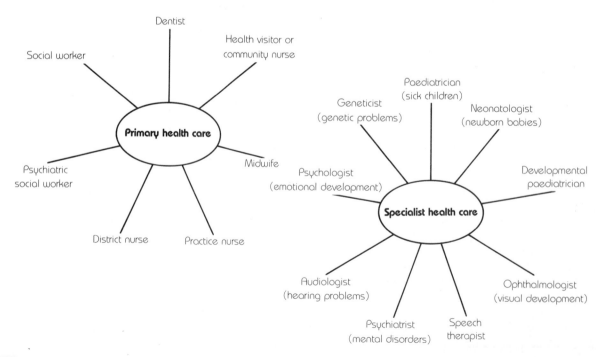

Handicapped children must be treated as normally as the handicap will allow.

They will need love, security, companionship, opportunities to develop, discipline and good physical care.
They will not need over-protecting, pity, to have everything done for them, constant sympathy, over pressuring and exclusion from the company of able-bodied children.

All children must be encouraged to reach their true potential and children with a handicap must be stretched and stimulated just as the able-bodied child is. The degree of handicap is important. The child with a slight abnormality may require little special treatment, but the more severely handicapped may require special:

- education
- diet
- medication
- transport
- therapy
- training
- house adaptations
- toys and activities.

It is important that:

- They are given opportunities and encouragement to integrate with able-bodied children.
- They are taught how to accept the unintentional or intentional stares, whispers and unkindness of others.
- They are helped to achieve a positive attitude towards themselves, rather than a negative one. This can only be done if parents, family and society also have this attitude.

Effects on the family

The birth of a handicapped child, or a child developing a handicap, is a traumatic experience for the family. For parents, the usual pattern is, tremendous shock and disbelief, followed by resentment, guilt and finally acceptance. Some parents never accept a handicapped child and he or she may have to be adopted or taken into care.

For some families the situation will always be stressful and cause unhappiness; for others it is an enriching experience and encourages the development of caring attitudes, bringing the family closer together. Some parents feel shame, embarrassment, guilt, frustration or even hate. These negative feelings set a poor example for other siblings to follow. Grandparents and other relations may also be embarrassed, show no concern or squabble over where the 'blame' for the handicap lies. However, most families are supportive. Handicapped children are usually best cared for in their own homes and it is usually the mother who has the main responsibility for the child and accepts this as her role. Most fathers go out to work and give only intermittent help with the easier aspects of caring. Therefore the mother bears much of the strain and needs a lot of support.

Problems causing stress in the family in this situation include:

- marital difficulties
- jealousy in siblings
- financial problems
- overwork for the mother
- housing problems
- isolation
- rejection by some relations
- lack of opportunities for social or recreational activities.

It is important therefore that family support is given in the form of:

- Visits from health visitors and social workers.
- Expert counselling, if required.
- Readily available information on statutory benefits and aids.
- Good educational provision from an early age.
- Progressive testing and treatment for the child.
- Day care or residential care if needed.
- Opportunities for social mixing.
- Enlightened and caring attitudes from the community.

Help available

Community support

Statutory benefits are:

1. **Financial** Child benefit;
   (possibly) attendance allowance;
   invalid care allowance; mobility
   allowance; income support/family
   credit; transport allowance for
   hospital visiting; free transport to
   school; day-care centre,
   allowances towards clothing,
   food, heating.

2. **Health** Free medical care, NHS
   prescriptions, dental and optical
   services; milk and vitamins (low
   income); specialist care and
   treatment, therapy and
   hospitalisation, immunisation and
   developmental testing; specially
   trained paediatricians, therapists,
   teachers, psychologists, social
   workers, special aids and
   equipment such as wheelchairs
   and callipers.

3. **Education and day care**
   Allocation of places in
   playgroups, nursery classes, day-
   care centres, special schools – day
   or residential, or special units
   attached to school. School care
   assistants to help individual
   children. Advisory teachers of the
   blind or severely handicapped.

4. **Social** Home helps, laundry
   services, child minders; family
   centres, special clubs, holiday
   centres; short-term fostering;
   riding and swimming facilities;
   special housing.

   Many of the benefits suggested in
   3 and 4 are provided by local
   authorities and are therefore not
   available in all areas. LAs who
   are bad at providing these
   facilities should be pressurised
   into doing so.

Voluntary support
(brief selection only)

1. **General help groups**
   CAB; Relate (formerly the
   Marriage Guidance Council);
   National Children's Home;
   Voluntary Council for
   Handicapped Children; Play
   Matters/National Toy Libraries
   Association; Disabled Living
   Foundation; Family Network;
   Community Health Councils.

2. **Specific voluntary help groups**
   Down's Children Association;
   Royal Society for Mentally
   Handicapped Children and Adults
   (MENCAP); The Spastics Society;
   Association of Vaccine Damaged
   Children; Family Fund; National
   Deaf Children's Society; Royal
   National Institute for the Blind
   (RNIB).

3. **Self-help groups**
   Contact a Family with a
   Handicapped Child; Parents
   Anonymous; National Association
   for the Welfare of Children in
   Hospital; Family Network (phone-
   in service); Prospect (campaign
   for parent's choice of treatment);
   National Blind–Deaf Helpers
   League; Compassionate Friends
   (support group for bereaved
   parents); Hyperactive Children's
   Support Group; Talking Books
   and Magazines for the Blind.

Pupil participation

Working briefs

1. Physical and mental handicaps

Group work (Triggers)

Hearing impaired

Down's syndrome

Physically disabled

Visual handicap

The children in these pictures are all handicapped in different ways. Find pictures of other types of handicap in books or magazines. Divide into groups to discuss the difficulties which can be faced by these children and suggest how they can be helped to achieve as much independence as possible.

2. Prevention of handicap

Group work (Role play)

Carry out some research on each of the following topics and then role play the situations.

a) Immunisation. Mother attending child health clinic with small baby, talking to clinic nurse:

'I think that David is due to be immunised soon, but my neighbour told me not to have him done, because she knows someone whose baby was left brain-damaged after he was vaccinated.'

b) Pregnancy tests. Pregnant woman attending antenatal clinic, talking to clinic doctor:

'I don't want to have a scan. Someone told me there is a risk of it causing a miscarriage, and as I've had one miscarriage I don't want to cause another.'

Think of further topics to discuss and role play.

3. Needs of the handicapped child

Problem-solving assignments

Although many toys will amuse handicapped children, they can also frustrate them. Well-designed toys and games to suit their needs can be expensive and hard to find.

Design brief Plan, design and make things suitable for the following:

a) A play-tray to attach to a wheelchair.
b) A game for a visually handicapped child.
c) A game suitable for integrating a wheelchair-bound child with able-bodied children.

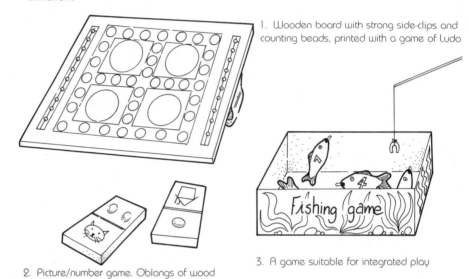

1. Wooden board with strong side-clips and counting beads, printed with a game of Ludo

2. Picture/number game. Oblongs of wood with raised, textured dots and pictures.

3. A game suitable for integrated play

Examples of toys for handicapped children

4. Aids for the handicapped child

Individual community work

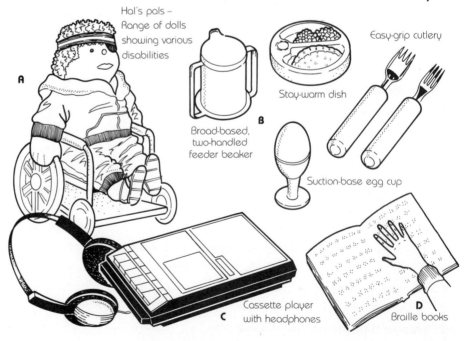

Hal's pals – Range of dolls showing various disabilities

A

Broad-based, two-handled feeder beaker

B

Stay-warm dish

Easy-grip cutlery

Suction-base egg cup

Cassette player with headphones

C

Braille books

D

Study these pictures and decide how these aids could help with certain handicaps. Copy the chart into your book and fill in the columns.

	Hal's pals	Tableware	Braille books	Cassette player
a) Which handicaps would be best catered for by its use?				
b) How would it be used?				
c) What are its advantages?				
d) Any disadvantages?				
e) Any similar items to aid the handicapped?				

(See example on page 153.)

5. Effects of handicap on the family   Group or individual

Consider the following problems and suggest some possible ways of dealing with them. Some examples are given.

Problem	Possibilities
a) 'I have a 4-year-old mentally handicapped child who needs constant attention. Although I love him very much, I get exhausted and tense with the work and worry. My husband is away for long periods and I get very lonely. Who can help?'	Contact your social services department for information about day care. Talk to your health visitor.
b) 'I have a young sister who is spastic and makes odd noises and gestures when we go out. People stare and I feel so embarrassed. My friends at school sometimes tease me. I love my sister, but I am beginning to feel ashamed of her. What can I do?'	Try to accept the guilt as it is a natural reaction. Contact the local branch of the Spastic Society, as discussing a problem often helps.
c) 'My child is partially deaf and wears a hearing aid. She recently started at our local primary school, where she is coping well, but some of the older children have already started to tease and bully her. Should I interfere at this stage?'	Contact the school for advice.

6. Community help   Class or individual

This is a familiar logo which symbolises physical handicaps and the places where handicapped people are catered for. Survey your local town. List the places where this sign appears. These should include shops, banks, theatres and cinemas; public buildings such as the town hall, public library, police station, public conveniences and leisure facilities. If you feel that access and provision for handicapped children and adults is insufficient, contact your local town council, MP or newspaper, asking why.

7. Voluntary help   Individual or group

Make up a **fact file** containing information about several of the voluntary organisations mentioned on page 134. Don't forget to send a stamped addressed envelope if you write to them for information. As a follow-up project:

a) Try to entertain a handicapped child in your home, or produce an entertainment for a group from a local school for handicapped children.
b) Plan and carry out a fund-raising event for a local handicap society.
c) Offer your help in reading to the blind, take out a child in a wheelchair, or help at riding stables for handicapped children. Your local Volunteer Bureau should be able to give suggestions.

Keep a record of your activities and illustrate them with photographs and drawings.

Written work

Fact finding exercise

1.

Condition	Possible Symptoms
	Slanting eyes, flat nose, small mouth, curved fingers.
Coeliac disease	
	A baby who does not turn towards sound or jump at loud noises.
Rickets	
	Blood which does not clot.
Cerebral palsy	
	Breathing difficulties, cough, short of breath.
Cleft palate	

a) Copy this chart into your book.
b) Fill in the boxes.
c) State briefly what is being done and what can be done to help children with these handicaps.

2. Explain the following terms:
sensory handicaps   interrelated handicaps   viral infections
retarded development   the Agpar score.

3. Find out about, and write a paragraph on:

SCBUs (special care baby units).

The Guthrie test.

The advantages of an early diagnosis of handicap.

Environment and handicap.

The role of the health visitor in dealing with handicapped children.

Application of knowledge

1. Some handicapped children need to spend long periods of time in hospital. Explain how:

   a) Contact with home and family can be maintained.

   b) Normal developmental progress can be encouraged where possible.

   c) The doll shown in the picture is specially designed to have parts such as heart, lungs and appendix which can be taken out; muscles and bone layers, etc. How can a teaching doll like this be used to give confidence?

2. A child can look perfectly able-bodied but have a 'hidden' handicap. List some handicaps which are not obvious and suggest ways in which other people may be made aware of the related problems.

Problem solving

Parents are usually the first to notice lack of progress in a child's development. In which of the circumstances shown below should a parent seek help, and why? Which specialists can help?

a) A 3-year-old who has difficulty getting words out and has started stammering.

b) A 5-year-old who is still wetting the bed at night.

c) A 12-month-old child who does not move around unaided.

d) A 2- to 3-year-old whose general development is retarded and not at the level of others at her age.

Data response

Study the toys shown in the picture.

A Play intercom phones

B Doctor's set

D Plastic playball

E Balloon squeakers

F Sand and water play trays

C Voice activated toy – when
apple is spoken to,
the worm pops up.

1. Which of the toys would help to encourage social play between handicapped
   and non-handicapped chidren?

2. Why would toy D be of special value to the visually handicapped?

3. What safety points would you consider for toy E?

4. Which toys will especially encourage speech development? Give reasons.

5. What are toy libraries? How can they be a special help to handicapped
   children and their parents?

Free response

1. Discuss the advantages and the shortcomings of the following methods of
   educating handicapped children. Suggest which types of handicap and age
   group would be best suited by each method.
   a) Residential schools for the disabled.
   b) Day special schools.
   c) Special units attached to schools for able-bodied children.
   d) Home tuition.

2. 'Handicapped children tend to be the subject of favouritism on the part of
   parents and therefore jealousy on the part of siblings.'

   Discuss this statement and show how parents of a handicapped child can
   retain family unity.

Self-assessment

Photocopy and complete the self-assessment chart on page 161, inserting the following topics under 'The work I have done includes':

1. Definitions of physical handicaps
2. Definitions of mental handicaps
3. Causes
4. Diagnosis
5. Prevention
6. Treatment
7. Personnel involved
8. Needs of the handicapped child
9. Effects on the family
10. Community help available
11. Voluntary help available.

Photocopy and complete the self-marking plan on page 162 for the seven working briefs in this unit.

Study Area 3

Child Abuse and Alternative Families

Child abuse

Some facts

A child who has been physically or mentally abused can be scarred for life. Children are at risk from:

- physical ill-treatment
- neglect
- sexual abuse
- mental or emotional ill-treatment.

Child cruelty usually takes place in the child's home and is practised by parents, step-parents, older siblings or relations. Sometimes cases are reported in residential homes and schools, or homes other than the child's own. Neighbours or strangers are often involved, especially in sexual abuse.

Much abuse, such as neglect, physical abuse or isolation, takes place over a long period and sometimes ill-treatment is the result of parents losing patience, with disastrous results.

In 1985 64 children under 5 years were killed by parents or carers.
26 children under 2 years were abandoned.
633 cases of gross indecency with a child were reported.
277 cases of incest were reported.

E & W Criminal Statistics

These are only some of the reported cases. It is estimated that there are approximately 50 000 unreported cases of child abuse every year.

Causes of child abuse

The main reasons for child abuse are:

- Stress in the home caused by: marital problems; financial problems; housing problems; unemployment; very large families; handicapped parents.
- Immature, inexperienced parents.
- Parents who come from disturbed home backgrounds.
- Parents who are drug addicts or bullies.
- Parents who expect too much of their children.
- Children who are unwanted or have a long separation from their parents or have a handicap.

Parents who commit abuse can come from any socio-economic group.

Recognition and effects

Adults who deal with young children such as clinic nurses, doctors, teachers and social workers, should be suspicious of signs which can indicate child abuse, although many of the signs of abuse listed have other causes. Signs of abuse may be seen in a child who:

- Is underdeveloped and undernourished.
- Is dirty and has a neglected appearance.

- Has bruising, burns, scalds or other physical injuries.
- Has retarded speech or speech problems.
- Shows abnormal behaviour; for example, is over-aggressive, bullying, sullen or uses bad language.
- Is listless, nervous, withdrawn or defensive or who flinches.

Child abuse can lead to: nervous disorders, severe physical disabilities, inability to socialise and make friends, insecurity and unhappiness, inability to make close, loving relationships in adult life and a continuation of the abuse syndrome into the child's own adult family life.

Some results of abuse are visible, but emotional scars are unseen and can be just as damaging.

Prevention

Some methods of prevention include:

- Education in: schools; training courses for medical personnel; ante- and postnatal clinics; magazines, newspapers and TV coverage.
- Encouraging close family bonding and relationships.

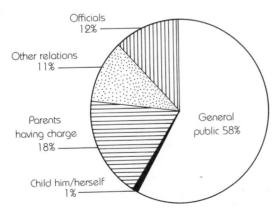

Officials 12%

Other relations 11%

Parents having charge 18%

Child him/herself 1%

General public 58%

NSPCC

Source of NSPCC information on child abuse, 1988

- Provision of good statutory help, for example, financial or housing help and day care for young chidren, is necessary, especially for problem families with children at risk.
- Counselling, contraceptive advice, etc., from community and voluntary services.
- Detection – suspected cases **must** be reported to the police, NSPCC, social worker or any other responsible person. The NSPCC dealt with 23 175 referrals involving 45 713 cases of child abuse between October 1986 and September 1987. The pie chart on page 143 shows how they received their information.

Help available

These agencies may be contacted if a case of child abuse is suspected.

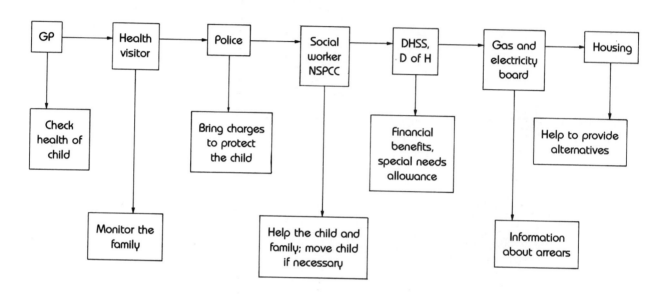

The child or children may be moved to an alternative family if considered to be in danger, but every effort is made to keep children in their own family if possible. It is usually better to give the family support than to split them up.

Children in problem families may be put on an 'at risk' file. They will then be constantly checked and monitored by social workers.

The government gives stiff sentences and treatment to child molestors. An amendment to the New Children's Bill being considered (in 1989) could require parents to produce a child, considered at risk from abuse, for medical examination within three days. Child pornography laws are being tightened up.

Young children are being taught how to help themselves with organisations such as Kidscape – the national campaign for children's safety – and Childline – the telephone service which can be rung by children in danger. Local authorities have their own schemes. The constable in the photograph is sent into schools to get over the message of 'stranger danger'.

Voluntary agencies (some with government support) such as the NSPCC, National Children's Home, Barnardos and The Church of England Children's Society will try to rehabilitate and support the families or give them a short period of time without the child so that they can assess their problems. Many of them support drop-in and walk-in centres, counselling services and education and advisory services, and carry out development and research.

Beware . . . stranger danger!

Alternative families

When children have an unsatisfactory home background or are left without parental care, temporarily or permanently, it is necessary to put them into an alternative family situation.

Children in care

Children in need of care are either **received** or **committed** into care. Children under 18 are **received** into care, usually at the request of a parent, for the following reasons:

- Short- or long-term illness of parent.
- Illness, death or confinement of the mother or father.
- Family homelessness, or having an unsatisfactory home.
- Being abandoned, lost or deserted.
- Having a parent in prison.

There were 30 890 children received for these reasons in 1984 in England and Wales (DHSS, 1984).

Children are **committed** into care through a care order instigated by the police, local authority or NSPCC for the following reasons:

- Neglect, or ill-treatment.
- Member of the family being convicted of an offence against the child.
- Moral danger or beyond parental control, or not receiving full-time education.
- Being guilty of an offence – commital is then in place of a supervision order.

There were 32 746 children committed for these reasons in 1984 in England and Wales (DHSS, 1984).

Of the 12-million child population (under 18) in England and Wales in 1984, 78 889 were in care (Hansard). The total number of children in care or under supervision in Scotland in 1984 was 13 783.

Provisions

Children in need of care are usually:

- Placed in a residential home – local authority or voluntary.
- Boarded out, that is, placed in a foster home.
- Adopted.
- Taken into the home of relatives or friends.
- If handicapped, placed in special schools or homes for the handicapped.

Professional people responsible for the care of children will always try to keep children with their families when possible and give family support. Local authority and voluntary agencies provide drop-in centres, day centres, family centres, playgroups, mother and toddler groups, holiday schemes, counselling and temporary care to take the pressure off stressed families. It is often possible for the child to be retained in the family group with supervision from a social worker. Residential homes set up by the LA and voluntary societies are run in small, family units, taking children for temporary care, or those who are difficult to foster or adopt. The old idea of orphanages is now very dated.

Adoption and fostering

There are fewer babies and young children now available for fostering and adoption because of:

- better contraception • greater availability of abortion • less stigma attached to illegitimacy • better social help for single mothers – one child in five is now born out of wedlock, but many are kept by the unmarried parent(s).

The children available for adoption in the UK now tend to be:

- older children and teenagers • sibling groups • non-white children
- children with mental or physical handicaps or emotional problems.

In 1986, there were 7892 adoptions; in 1976, there were 17 621. There are 27 000 foster parents in Britain, providing homes for 44 per cent of children in care.

Fostering facts

- Fostering is usually a short-term arrangement.
- Foster parents are paid a boarding-out allowance to cover the child's keep. Some local authorities pay a salary to foster parents who take especially difficult cases.
- Foster parents have no legal rights over the children, who can be removed at any time.
- Children are fostered through local authorities or voluntary agencies. It is seen as an ideal alternative to residential care.
- Some fostering agencies advertise their children in local newspapers or on TV. They may keep a book of profiles of the children available.
- Many foster children have emotional problems due to a troubled background and separation from parents. They require special understanding and patience. Training courses and group meetings are available for foster parents.
- Foster parents can come from any cultural or socio-economic background. They can be married, single, divorced, young or old. Agencies will try to match a child to suitable foster parents.
- There are several categories – short-term, long-term, intermediate; specialist foster parents for children with physical or mental handicaps, or older or younger children; holiday foster parents; weekend foster homes through the 'Links' and 'Respite Care' schemes.
- Fostering does not have the commitment of adoption, but provides a loving atmosphere for children in need. Few adoptions result from fostering, as that is not the purpose.
- People who wish to foster children should approach their local authority, a voluntary society such as Barnardos or the National Foster Care Association.

Adoption facts

- Adoption is a legal commitment. The natural parents lose all rights over the child when the adoption is finalised.
- People wishing to adopt a child should approach an approved adoption agency run by the local authority or a voluntary society. British Agencies for Adoption and Fostering (BAAF) produces an annual guide, Adopting a Child. Private adoptions are illegal except between close relatives.
- A child is placed with a family for at least three months as a probationary period; the prospective adoptive parents then apply for an adoption order and, after a court hearing at which social workers present reports, the adoption may be legalised.
- The natural parents' consent is needed before an adoption order is approved, except in certain circumstances. Sometimes one parent's consent is sufficient.
- It is usually recommended that proposed adopters should be over 21 years old and probably below 40; be in good health; usually be married; be of the same ethnic and religious group as the child(ren); have a mature outlook and be fond of children; and have satisfactory home conditions.
- Once approved, the adoption is legal and cannot be reversed. The parents get all the usual state benefits such as child allowance.

Effects on the child and the family

Although every effort is made to match children to suitable families, problems do sometimes occur afterwards. Older children in particular may find it difficult to settle down. Other children in the family may become jealous; foster parents may not be able to cope with problem children; **or** the child may miss his or her natural parents and family and have feelings of guilt and resentment.

The problem of when and how to tell children that they are adopted worries many parents, and learning this fact is often traumatic for the child. The 1975 Children's Act made it possible for adopted children to have access to their original birth certificates and trace their natural parents. The Post-Adoption Centre provides professional support and advice in these circumstances.

Foster children who do not fit into the foster family may have several moves. This can be unsettling and make the child feel a failure and insecure. Although many children placed in alternative family care grow up into well-adjusted adults, a number have difficulties with relationships in later life.

Pupil participation ———————————

Working briefs

1. Child abuse   Individual or class work (Case histories)

Case history 1.   Bob and June are a young couple who live together in a small council flat which is damp and poorly furnished. Neither is employed and Bob has been involved in petty crime. They have a baby of 6 months who is never taken to the baby clinic. On one occasion when the health visitor called, she noticed that June had bruising on her face and the baby had a cut lip and bruising on her body. June said the child had fallen downstairs. The flat was dirty and cold and there seemed to be no food about.

Case history 2.   The playgroup leader notices that Jenny has a neglected appearance, is thin, quiet and listless and rarely smiles. She reports this to the community social worker, who calls on the family. She finds that the mother lives in a warm, comfortable, well-furnished house and has two other happy, healthy children. There is no sign of Jenny and her mother makes an excuse to explain her absence.

Case history 3. The Kainth family lives next door to Lynn, who is a single parent with three young children. Lynn's house looks dirty and the children appear neglected. For several nights Mr and Mrs Kainth have been woken by the children crying and screaming, often as late as 2 a.m. They suspect that Lynn is going out and leaving the children alone.

What could be happening in each of these situations? In each case, what action do you think should be taken? List the support services available to help the families.

2. Sexual abuse
Individual (Collaborative learning game)

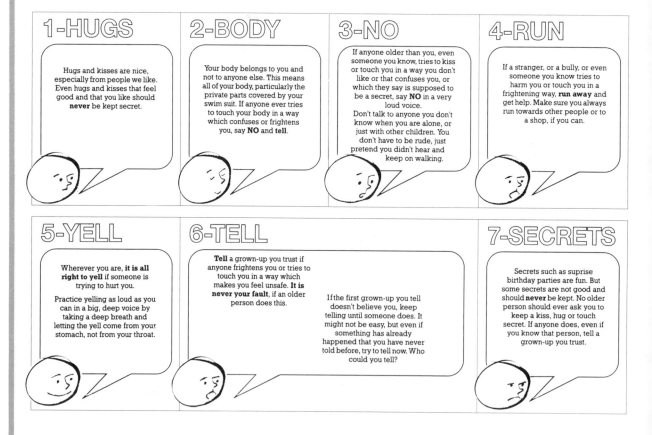

1-HUGS

Hugs and kisses are nice, especially from people we like. Even hugs and kisses that feel good and that you like should **never** be kept secret.

2-BODY

Your body belongs to you and not to anyone else. This means all of your body, particularly the private parts covered by your swim suit. If anyone ever tries to touch your body in a way which confuses or frightens you, say **NO** and **tell**.

3-NO

If anyone older than you, even someone you know, tries to kiss or touch you in a way you don't like or that confuses you, or which they say is supposed to be a secret, say **NO** in a very loud voice.
Don't talk to anyone you don't know when you are alone, or just with other children. You don't have to be rude, just pretend you didn't hear and keep on walking.

4-RUN

If a stranger, or a bully, or even someone you know tries to harm you or touch you in a frightening way, **run away** and get help. Make sure you always run towards other people or to a shop, if you can.

5-YELL

Wherever you are, **it is all right to yell** if someone is trying to hurt you.

Practice yelling as loud as you can in a big, deep voice by taking a deep breath and letting the yell come from your stomach, not from your throat.

6-TELL

Tell a grown-up you trust if anyone frightens you or tries to touch you in a way which makes you feel unsafe. **It is never your fault**, if an older person does this.

If the first grown-up you tell doesn't believe you, keep telling until someone does. It might not be easy, but even if something has already happened that you have never told before, try to tell now. Who could you tell?

7-SECRETS

Secrets such as suprise birthday parties are fun. But some secrets are not good and should **never** be kept. No older person should ever ask you to keep a kiss, hug or touch secret. If anyone does, even if you know that person, tell a grown-up you trust.

The Keepsafe Code, part of which is illustrated above, has been devised by Kidscape to teach children 'Good Sense Defence'. Assess its value. Is the message clear? Find out more about the activities of Kidscape (the address is on page 160). For practical work, design and produce the following to get the child-abuse message across to children:

a) A poster or wall frieze for a child's bedroom or the playgroup wall.
b) A board game or jigsaw.
c) An illustrated slogan.

(See example on page 154.)

3. Child abuse — Class work (Triggers)

'Each child brought to me blind or paralysed from battering gives rise to feelings of revulsion and despair, and yet in my experience well over half the children brought to court as a result of ill-treatment are returned home.'

Brenda Farman, head of an NCH home for handicapped and abused children

Use this extract to start a discussion on the care of abused children and family training and rehabilitation.

4. Child abuse — Individual work (Problem solving)

1. Man in car offers lift

2. Sweater or satchel with child's name on

3. Lonely short-cut to home from school

4. Babysitter says 'Let's keep it a secret'

These pictures show potentially dangerous situations for children.

a) Explain what the dangers could be.
b) How would you explain these dangers to a child?
c) Write down and illustrate some further potentially dangerous situations.

5. Alternative families — Group work (Investigation)

Divide into three groups.
Group 1. Children's homes. **Group 2.** Fostering **Group 3.** Adoption.
Within your groups gather information about your given subject. Produce an information pack about each type of alternative family, including where possible pictures, statistics and local information. List and discuss the positive and negative aspects of each system.

6. Adoption and fostering

Individual or class work (fact file)

LOUISE was four years old when she arrived at Pam and Keith Oiller's Victorian terraced house in Kent.

"She was a pretty little girl. She looked perfectly normal, like any other four year old," said Pam.

She wasn't. Louise didn't like being hugged, she was terrified of the sounds of the Hoover, the hair drier and Keith's electric shaver. She hated bath times and she got very depressed.

"She would sit on the couch and just cry for 20 minutes for no apparent reason. Sometimes she would hide herself in a cupboard in my daughter's room, and I'd find her hugging her doll and saying, 'There, there, don't cry, it's all right now baby, you're safe now baby.'"

Eventually, the truth came out. Louise was sitting in the bath one night when she told her foster mother just how she had been sexually abused. "I knew that was the turning point. I felt I'd done my job," said Pam.

ANDREW, 29, has a long, rebellious history behind him. His adoptive parents sent him to public school, from which he ran away to start a wandering, unsettled life. He has never had a job but moved from one vague project to another, succeeding at nothing.

Last year, taking advantage of the rights given to adopted children under the Children's Act, 1975, by which they have access to their original birth certificates, he traced his real mother. They met on a bridge over the Thames in the London rush-hour. Andrew says he knew who his mother was the minute he saw her in the crowd.

He learned that as a scholarship student, she had a brief affair with a young German, became pregnant but felt quite unable to keep her baby. "Now, at last, I really know who I am," he says. They meet regularly.

These two newspaper cuttings are about people involved in adoption and fostering. In both cases the situation turned out well. The endings could have been different. What problems could have arisen in both cases, and what advice and help would have been available? Try to find other such accounts in newspapers and magazines and make up a fact file of relevant cases. Analyse them to discover the strengths and weaknesses of our system of alternative family care.

7. Fostering

Class work (Rounds)

'The qualities and skills needed to make good foster parents are . . .'
'Because . . .'
Suggest some qualities or skills, needed to make good foster parents, for example, being imaginative, being lively, caring, having practical skills and give good reasons for your choices.
Do this with everyone in the class giving an opinion. It will improve your verbal skills.

Written work

Fact finding exercise

1. Write a paragraph about each of the following:
   The legal requirements for a registered child minder.
   The setting up of a Childline.
   The Marie Cauldwell or Jasmine Beckford case.
   How to arrange an adoption.

2. Find out about and write a detailed account on the work of one of the following:
   British Agencies for Adoption and Fostering, NSPCC, Parents Anonymous.

Application of knowledge

1. Explain the terms:

   Socio-economic groups   marital problems   voluntary care
   a care order   'at risk' file   family rehabilitation

2. Farida is a handicapped baby a few weeks old who has been abandoned by her parents.
   Anne's mother will be in hospital for two to three months, her father is working abroad and the family have no close relatives.
   Clive is a hyperactive child, putting his parents under a lot of stress. The social worker finds that they have been physically ill-treating him.
   Look at the options available for temporary or permanent care, on page 146.
   Which would you suggest for the cases listed above, and why?

Free response

1. Adoption agencies try to place children for adoption in families of the same cultural background. Suggest reasons for this and express your own views on the subject.

2. Give examples of physical and emotional abuse of children and contrast the damage which can result from both types of abuse.

Data response

This chart shows the ages of the children dealt with in child abuse cases by the NSPCC.

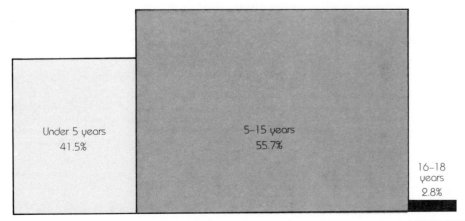

Under 5 years
41.5%

5–15 years
55.7%

16–18 years
2.8%

NSPCC 1986

1. Which age group has the highest percentage of child abuse cases?

2. Suggest three reasons why over 40 per cent of cases are in the under-five age group.

3. Most cases of child abuse are caused by family stress, not deliberate cruelty. Give five examples of stress situations which could lead to child abuse.

4. Give detailed accounts of two campaigns which are aimed at reducing child abuse and giving help to abused children and their families.

Self-assessment

Photocopy and complete the self-assessment chart on page 161, inserting the following topics under 'The work I have done includes':

Child abuse:
1. Facts
2. Causes
3. Recognition and effects
4. Prevention
5. Help available

Alternative families:
1. Children in care
2. Provision
3. Adoption and fostering
4. Effects.

Photocopy and complete the self-marking plan on page 162 for the seven working briefs in this unit.

Appendices – Study Area 3

Methods of presenting and recording results

Family life (page 111)

Example 1.   Social services (page 125)
Informative posters Brief – to design a poster clearly explaining the benefits available for certain groups of the community. Examples chosen:

1. A poster suitable for display in the social services office, public library, post office or doctor's waiting room, drawing attention to the benefits available and how to collect them.

2. A poster suitable for display in a child clinic, antenatal clinic, CAB office, etc., drawing attention to family benefits.

Plan your poster. It should be clear, informative, colourful and eye-catching.
Try out something different – graffiti style, pop art or collage.
Make your poster.
Test it out on your friends.
Evaluate Does it get the message over? How could it be improved?

Handicaps (page 129)

Example 2. Aids for the handicapped child (pages 136–7)
Collate the information you have gathered together and present it in the form of a pictogram, as shown in example 1. Other information can be shown as bar charts, as in example 2. Analyse the results of your charts.

① Pictogram to show which handicaps would most benefit from the use of the four aids shown

	A	B	C	D
Physical handicaps	♿♿	♿♿		
Visual handicaps	♿	♿	♿	♿♿♿
Auditory handicaps			♿♿	
Speech defects			♿♿	
Retarded development	♿		♿	
Brain damage	♿	♿	♿	
Total	♿♿♿♿♿	♿♿♿♿	♿♿♿♿♿♿♿	♿♿♿

Key_

A = Hal's pals
B = Tableware
C = Braille books
D = Cassette
         player

Key: ♿   The higher the number of symbols the greater benefit obtained from the aid

② Disadvantages

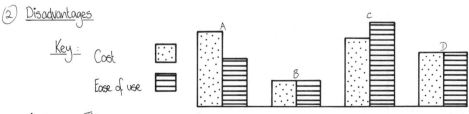

Key: Cost
        Ease of use

Analysis: The tape recorder, although quite expensive and complicated to use could
be of benefit for most types of handicap.

Child abuse and alternative families (page 142)

Example 3.   Sexual abuse (page 148)

Learning game Design brief – to design and construct a toy or game to help make children aware of dangers from strangers.

Aims It should be simple to understand, easy to play, colourful, interesting, safe and fun to play.

Restrictions It should not frighten or confuse the child; it should be quite cheap; the child is under 5 years and therefore limited in reasoning powers.

Ideas Look in children's comics, magazines or toy catalogues. An idea is given below. It could be extended by cutting out the shapes of the boy, the symbols and the word and using them as drop-in jigsaw shapes.

Materials Thick card, plywood, felt, poster paints, felt pens, varnish, embroidery thread, etc.

Safety Non-toxic, non-splinter, no small bits and no other aspects which could be hazardous to small children.

Make up the design.

Evaluation

Does it work?

Does the child understand it?

Is it fun and interesting?

Could you improve on your design, or is it successful as it is?

1. A man in a car asks Sammy if he would like to go for an ice cream.
2. A big boy asks Sammy to help him find his dog.
3. A strange lady says she has come to take him home from school.
4. Sammy has lost his ball in the wood. A man in the park offers to help him look for it.

WHAT MUST SAMMY SAY?

A safety game

Resources guide

Family life

Leaflets and booklets	Publisher or source
'From the Cradle to the Grave'	Documentary Division, Yorkshire TV.
Assorted leaflets on housing problems	Shelter
Assorted leaflets on social security benefits	Child Poverty Action Group
'How to help children through divorce' leaflet	Mediation in Divorce
'Interventions', multi-cultural learning pack	Save the Children
'Family Finances', 'One-Parent Families', 'The Family Today', 'Family Policy Bulletin'	Family Policy Studies Centre
'Children in Danger', National Children's Home (NCH)fact file	NCH
'Reforming Social Security', Fact Sheets, 'Which Benefit', 'Maternity Benefits', etc.	DSS, Leaflets Unit
'Adopting a Child', annual guide, 'Child Care Law'	British Association for Adoption and Fostering (BAAF)
'A Guide to Care Proceedings'	Family Rights Group
Leaflets on fostering	National Foster Care Association
Leaflets and films	Barnardos
'The Family', resource pack, 'Life Skills Training Manual'	Community Service Volunteers
'Buying and Selling Your Home' and many other leaflets	Halifax Building Society
'The Money Issue', worksheets	The Building Societies Association
'Shopping Value'	The Direct Selling Association
'60 Years of Product Reliability', 'Playing Safe with British Standards'	BSI Public Relations Dept
Audio tapes on health and social services, such as 'Maternity Care', 'Social Services Problems'	Healthline Service

Handicaps

Films	Source
Immunisation Series – a lifetime of protection	CFL Vision
Immunisation – Five trigger films, also in Welsh, free loan	CFL Vision and Concord Films Council

Leaflets and booklets	Publisher or source
'Sound Advice', 'Can't Talk Yet?' 'Heart Disease and Mental Health', etc.	Health Education Council (HEC)
School pack, posters, leaflets	British Diabetic Association
'In Our Own Right; beyond the label of physical disability'. 'Insight: mental illness in perspective'	Community Service Volunteers

'The Child with a Medical Problem in the Ordinary School; children with special needs'	Home and School Council
'Talk' and other leaflets	The National Deaf Children's Society
'What is Cerebral Palsy?'	The Spastics Society
'Health Care in the Home', 'Personal Care'	Boots
'Talking Sense'	National Deaf, Blind and Rubella Association

Department of Social Security leaflets
Almost all of the voluntary societies will provide relevant information.

Magazine	**Publisher**
Practical Health	Family Circle Publications

Teaching packs	**Publisher or source**
'Genetic Risk', to develop understanding about inherited disorders	Philip Harris Biological
'The Rubella Action Pack'	Sense

Video	**Source**
Roll On, issues affecting the disabled	Community Service Volunteers

Films	**Source**
Somebody Cares (Housing Associations), *Look at the Label*, *Page Three Story* (Credit buying), etc.	CFL Vision

Child abuse – alternative families

Leaflets and booklets	**Publisher or source**
'Children in Danger' pack, 'Children in Danger' fact file, etc.	NCH
'Protect Your Child', 'How the NSPCC Works', etc.	NSPCC
'Kidscape Code', 'Kidscape teaching pack', 'Safely home', board game	Kidscape
Newsletter and information from British Association for the Study and Prevention of Child Abuse and Neglect	Jacob Bright's Children's Centre
'Strong Kids, Safe Kids'	NCH

Video	**Source**
Children in Danger	NCH

Books

Title	**Publisher**
The Baby and Child Book, A. and P. Stanway	Pan Paperbacks
A Guide to Benefits for Handicapped Children and their Families, A. Cooper	Disability Alliance

Keeping Safe – A Practical Guide for Talking with Children, M. Elliot	Bedford Square Press
Maternity Rights Handbook, R. Evans and L. Durward	Penguin
Inside the Family: Changing Roles of Men and Women, M. Henwood, L. Rimmer, M. Wicks	Family Policy Studies Centre
Come and Tell Me, M. Hollick	Dinosaur
The Development of the Infant and Young Child Abnormal and Normal, R.S. Illingworth	Churchill Livingstone
The Other Side of Paediatrics, J. Jolly	Macmillan
Parents and the Handicapped Child – A Guide for Families, M. Marshall	Macrae Books
A Practical Guide to Child Development, Vol. 2, V. Reynolds	Stanley Thornes (Publishers) Ltd
Yours By Choice – A Guide for Adoptive Parents, J. Rowe	Routledge and Kegan Paul
Learning to Care in the Community, P. Turton and J. Orr	Hodder and Stoughton
A Handbook of Consumer Law (Which?)	Consumers' Association, Hodder and Stoughton
It's OK to say No!, colouring book, and *It's OK to say No!*, activity book	NCH
Key Data	Central Statistical Office, HMSO
National Welfare Benefits Handbook	Child Poverty Action Group
The Good Toy Guide	Play Matters/AC Black
The Human Body	Gallery Press
List of books on child abuse, neglect and its effects	NSPCC

Useful addresses

Study Area 1
Association for Improvement in the Maternity Services, 163 Liverpool Road,
London N1 0RF
Birth Centre, 101 Tufnell Park Road, London N7
Caesarean Support Groups, 9 Nightingale Grove, London SE13 6EY
Community Health Group for Ethnic Minorities, 28 Churchfield Road,
London W3 6EB
Foundation for the Study of Infant Deaths, 4 Grosvenor Place, London SW1
Harringtons, General Wolfe House, High Street, Westerham, Kent TN16 1RE
Hopscotch, 251 Brixton Road, London SW9
La Leche League, Box 3424, London WC1 6XX
National Rubella Council, 105 Gower Street, London NW1
National Childbirth Trust, Alexandra House, Oldham Terrace, Acton, London W3 6NH
Oh/One/Oh, Bradford, West Yorkshire BD99 4BR
Predictor, Cambridge Science Park, Milton Road, Cambridge CB4 4BH
Sterling Health, Sterling Winthrop House, Onslow Street, Guildford GU1 4VS
Tacade, 3rd Floor, Furness House, Trafford Road, Salford M5 2XJ
Twins Clubs Association, 27 Woodham Park Road, Weybridge, Surrey

Study Area 2
Book Trust, Book House, 45 East Hill, London SW18 2QZ
British Association for Early Childhood Education, 140 Tabernacle Street,
London EC2A 4SD
College of Speech Therapists, Harold Poster House, 6 Lechmere Road,
London NW2 5BU
Community Service Volunteers, 237 Pentonville Road, London N1
Fairy Tales (DTP Package), Resource, Exeter Road, Doncaster
Knitting Craft Group, PO Box 6, Thirsk, North Yorkshire YO7 1TA
Ladybird Books, PO Box 12, Beeches Road, Loughborough, Leicestershire LE11 2NQ
Macdonald 3/4/5 Nursery Course, Macdonald Educational, Holywell House,
Worship Street, London EC2
National Childminding Association, 8 Masons Hill, Bromley BR2 9EY
Robinsons Baby Foods, Carrow, Norwich NR1 2DD
RoSPA, Cannon House, The Priory Queensway, Birmingham B4 6BS
Under Five Magazine, 92 Queensway, Bletchley, Milton Keynes MK2 2QV

Study Area 3
Association for Spina Bifida and Hydrocephalus (ASBAH), 22 Upper Woburn Place,
London WC1H 0EP
BAAF, 11 Southwark Street, London SE1
Barnardos (PAO), Tanners Lane, Barkingside, Essex IG6 1QG
BSI Public Relations Department, 2 Park Street, London W1
British Diabetic Association, 10 Queen Anne Street, London W1
Building Societies Association, 3 Saville Row, London W1
Child Poverty Action Group, 1 Macklin Street, Drury Lane, London WC2
Community Service Volunteers, 237 Pentonville Road, London N1
DSS Leaflets Unit, PO Box 21 Stanmore, Middlesex HA7 1AY
Direct Selling Association, 44 Russell Square, London WC1
Disability Alliance, 25 Denmark Street, London WC2
Family Policy Studies Centre, 231 Baker Street, London W1

Family Rights Group, 6–9 Manor Gardens, Holloway Road, London N7 6LA

Halifax Building Society, Trinity Road, Halifax

Home and School Council, 81 Rustlings Road, Sheffield S11 7AB

Jacob Bright's Children's Centre, Whitechurch Road, Rochdale, Lancs.

Kidscape, 82 Brook Street, London W1Y 1YG

Mediation in Divorce, 13 Rosslyn Street, East Twickenham

NSPCC, 67 Saffron Hill, London EC1N 8RS

National Children's Home, 85 Highbury Park, London N5 1UD

National Deaf-Blind and Rubella Association, The Family Centre, 86 Cleveland Road, Ealing, London W13 0HE

National Deaf Children's Society, 45 Hereford Road, London

National Foster Care Association, Francis House, Francis Street, London

Philip Harris Biological, Oldmixon, Weston-super-Mare BS24 9BJ

Royal National Institute for the Blind, 224 Great Portland Street, London W1N 6AA

Royal National Institution for the Deaf, 105 Gower Street, London WC1E 6AH

Shelter, 155 Waterloo Road, London SE1

Spastics Society, 12 Park Crescent, London W1N 4EQ

Yorkshire TV, Documentary Division, The Television Centre, Leeds

SELF-ASSESSMENT CHART

Study area

_____

Unit

_____

Name _____

Date _____

Tick appropriate column:

☺ I am pleased with my work and covered at least one assignment. I feel confident that I know this area.

😐 I have completed most of this area of the work, but may need to go back for further revision.

☹ I am not happy with my work and must do more.

The work I have done includes:	☺	😐	☹	Working brief completed

I need to do more work on: _____

_____

I have visited: _____

_____

I need to visit: _____

_____

Books and resources used include: _____

_____

I have related some of this work to my child study/practical assignments/investigations: _____

_____

I found difficulty with parts of this unit because: _____

_____

Teacher's comments: _____

_____

Study area

SELF-MARKING PLAN – PRACTICAL ASSIGNMENTS

Unit

Name _____

Date _____

Analyse the skills you have used when working through the working briefs by ticking the appropriate skill on the chart below.

	Skills	Working Briefs												
		1	2	3	4	5	6	7	8	9	10	11	12	13
Practical, problem solving	Planning and organising													
	Gathering information													
	Developing ideas													
	Observing													
	Considering safety													
	Manipulative skills													
	Use of simple or complex equipment													
	Presentation of work													
Interpersonal	Working with others													
	Coping with changing situations													
	Being sensitive to the needs of others													
	Listening to others													
	Talking to others													
Personal, language and numeracy	Reading and understanding													
	Writing and recording information													
	Using signs, diagrams, technical terms													
	Accurate measuring of time, cost, area, temperature, distance, shape, size, quantity													
Investigational	Comprehension													
	Analysis													
	Interpretation of knowledge													
	Selection of relevant information													
	Decision making													
	Evaluation													

When you have completed your skills analysis, you will be able to see which skills you need to make more use of.

FINDING OUT ABOUT CHILD DEVELOPMENT	Common Elements			Common Themes						Skills						
	Home	Food	Textiles	Health	Safety and Protection	Efficiency	Values	Aesthetics	Interaction with Environment	Investigational	Measurement	Communication	Management	Psycho-motor	Technological	Interpersonal Caring
PRECONCEPTUAL CARE																
Reasons for planning ahead	✓	✓		✓	✓		✓		✓	✓		✓				
Children's basic needs	✓	✓	✓	✓	✓		✓				✓					✓
Stable relationships	✓			✓			✓			✓						✓
Housing	✓			✓	✓	✓		✓	✓	✓	✓	✓	✓			
Finance	✓	✓	✓			✓	✓	✓		✓	✓		✓			
Family roles				✓		✓	✓			✓		✓				✓
Diet		✓		✓	✓	✓			✓		✓	✓		✓	✓	
Exercise		✓		✓	✓	✓					✓			✓	✓	
Environmental	✓			✓	✓	✓	✓		✓	✓						✓
Alcohol, tobacco, drugs		✓		✓	✓		✓		✓	✓		✓				✓
Disease and infections	✓	✓		✓	✓					✓						✓
Chromosomes and genes		✓		✓	✓					✓	✓			✓	✓	
STDs				✓	✓							✓				✓
Inherited conditions	✓			✓	✓					✓		✓				✓
Stress	✓	✓		✓		✓			✓	✓	✓		✓			
BIOLOGICAL BACKGROUND	The information used for this unit is almost entirely to do with the main element of Child Development, the common elements having only a remote connection.															
Reproductive system				✓	✓					✓		✓				
Puberty				✓	✓							✓				✓
Menstruation				✓					✓			✓				✓
Fertilisation				✓	✓					✓						
Conception				✓						✓	✓					
Foetal development				✓	✓				✓	✓						
Multiple pregnancies				✓	✓				✓	✓						
PREGNANCY																
Reasons for care	✓	✓		✓	✓		✓		✓	✓						✓

FINDING OUT ABOUT CHILD DEVELOPMENT	Common Elements			Common Themes						Skills						
	Home	Food	Textiles	Health	Safety and Protection	Efficiency	Values	Aesthetics	Interaction with Environment	Investigational	Measurement	Communication	Management	Psycho-motor	Technological	Interpersonal Caring
Diet		✓		✓	✓	✓	✓	✓			✓	✓		✓		
Clothing			✓	✓	✓	✓	✓	✓	✓				✓	✓		
Rest and exercise	✓			✓			✓			✓						
Posture	✓			✓		✓		✓						✓		
Emotions	✓		✓	✓					✓	✓						
Father's role	✓	✓	✓	✓	✓	✓	✓			✓		✓				✓
Physical changes		✓		✓						✓	✓		✓			
Minor ailments		✓		✓					✓		✓			✓		
Medical care	✓			✓	✓	✓			✓						✓	✓
Antenatal clinic	✓	✓	✓	✓	✓	✓			✓	✓	✓		✓			
Tests				✓	✓							✓			✓	
Problems				✓	✓				✓	✓						✓
Baby's room	✓		✓	✓	✓	✓	✓	✓	✓		✓		✓			
Equipment	✓	✓	✓		✓	✓	✓	✓		✓		✓	✓			
Baby clothing			✓	✓	✓	✓	✓	✓	✓	✓	✓					
Preparations for birth	✓	✓				✓			✓		✓		✓			
BIRTH AND POSTNATAL CARE																
Stages of labour				✓	✓							✓				
Care during labour	✓	✓		✓	✓	✓										✓
Pain relief				✓		✓					✓			✓	✓	
Complications										✓		✓				
Postnatal care, mother & baby	✓	✓	✓	✓	✓	✓			✓			✓				✓
Postnatal tests, mother & baby				✓	✓	✓								✓	✓	
Feeding	✓		✓	✓	✓	✓	✓	✓	✓	✓						
Needs of new mother	✓	✓	✓	✓	✓			✓	✓							✓
Needs of new baby	✓	✓	✓	✓	✓			✓	✓	✓		✓		✓		

FINDING OUT ABOUT CHILD DEVELOPMENT	Common Elements			Common Themes						Skills						
	Home	Food	Textiles	Health	Safety and Protection	Efficiency	Values	Aesthetics	Interaction with Environment	Investigational	Measurement	Communication	Management	Psycho-motor	Technological	Interpersonal Caring
Hygiene	✓	✓	✓	✓	✓	✓	✓	✓	✓	✓			✓			
Routine	✓					✓	✓				✓		✓			
Crying		✓	✓	✓	✓				✓	✓		✓				✓

FINDING OUT ABOUT CHILD DEVELOPMENT	Common Elements			Common Themes						Skills						
	Home	Food	Textiles	Health	Safety and Protection	Efficiency	Values	Aesthetics	Interaction with Environment	Investigational	Measurement	Communication	Management	Psycho-motor	Technological	Interpersonal Caring
PHYSICAL DEVELOPMENT																
Physical growth	√	√		√	√				√	√	√					
Development of physical skills	√	√	√	√	√				√	√	√	√				
Sensory development	√			√	√					√	√					
Health and hygiene	√	√	√	√	√				√						√	√
Food		√		√	√	√	√	√			√		√	√		
Clothing			√	√	√	√	√	√	√		√			√		
Exercise and sleep	√			√		√				√						
Protection from disease	√	√	√	√	√	√			√	√	√					√
Safety and first aid	√			√	√	√			√	√						√
Play, toys and games	√	√	√	√	√	√	√	√		√			√			
INTELLECTUAL DEVELOPMENT																
Achievement of understanding	√									√	√					
Communication and language	√								√		√	√				
Stimuli: Environmental	√					√	√	√	√	√				√		
Stimuli: Parental	√					√	√		√					√		√
Toys and activities	√	√	√	√	√	√	√			√			√			
Books	√					√	√	√	√	√		√				
Educational provision	√	√	√						√				√		√	
SOCIAL & EMOTIONAL DEVELOPMENT																
Acquisition of social skills	√			√	√		√		√	√						
Pattern of social development	√	√					√		√	√		√				
Family relationships	√	√	√		√		√					√				√
Extended relationships	√	√	√		√		√			√						√
Behaviour and discipline	√	√	√		√		√		√	√			√			

FINDING OUT ABOUT CHILD DEVELOPMENT	Common Elements			Common Themes						Skills						
	Home	Food	Textiles	Health	Safety and Protection	Efficiency	Values	Aesthetics	Interaction with Environment	Investigational	Measurement	Communication	Management	Psycho-motor	Technological	Interpersonal Caring
Pattern of emotional development	√						√		√	√		√				
Emotional problems	√	√		√						√						√
Play	√			√	√		√		√			√		√		√

FINDING OUT ABOUT CHILD DEVELOPMENT	Common Elements			Common Themes						Skills						
	Home	Food	Textiles	Health	Safety and Protection	Efficiency	Values	Aesthetics	Interaction with Environment	Investigational	Measurement	Communication	Management	Psycho-motor	Technological	Interpersonal Caring
FAMILY AND COMMUNITY																
Family: Structures and functions	✓			✓	✓		✓			✓						✓
Family: Social change	✓	✓	✓	✓		✓				✓	✓					
Family: Finance and buying	✓	✓	✓	✓	✓	✓	✓	✓			✓		✓			
Family: Housing	✓			✓	✓			✓	✓	✓		✓	✓			✓
Community: Social Services	✓	✓	✓	✓	✓			✓	✓			✓				✓
Community: NHS	✓	✓		✓	✓	✓			✓	✓		✓				✓
Community: Voluntary organisations	✓			✓	✓	✓			✓	✓			✓			✓
HANDICAPS																
Physical and mental	✓			✓	✓				✓	✓			✓			
Causes	✓	✓		✓	✓				✓	✓	✓					
Diagnosis, prevention, treatment	✓	✓		✓	✓	✓			✓	✓	✓			✓	✓	
Personnel involved	✓			✓					✓	✓						✓
Needs of handicapped child	✓	✓	✓	✓	✓		✓	✓	✓		✓			✓		✓
Effects on family	✓			✓			✓		✓	✓		✓				✓
Community and voluntary help	✓					✓	✓		✓	✓		✓	✓			✓
CHILD ABUSE – ALTERNATIVE FAMILIES																
Child abuse: Facts	✓	✓	✓	✓	✓	✓			✓	✓		✓				
Child abuse: Causes	✓			✓	✓					✓						✓
Recognition and effects	✓			✓		✓			✓	✓						✓
Prevention	✓										✓	✓	✓			
Help available	✓				✓				✓			✓	✓			✓
Alternative families: In care	✓						✓			✓						✓
Alternative families: Provisions	✓			✓			✓		✓	✓	✓		✓			
Adoption and fostering	✓			✓			✓		✓				✓			✓
Adoption and fostering: Effects	✓			✓		✓				✓		✓				✓

Index

Page references in **bold** refer to pupil participation.

Finding Out About Child Development has been written to encourage active learning, and incorporates a high degree of student involvement. Students will expand on the core information provided for different topics by undertaking the many working briefs and written work exercises, which include: discussions, surveys, investigations, assignments, fact finding exercises, data response and free response questions.

The book provides guidance on the skills required for studying Child Development including methods of observing, investigating, recording and analysing information. It covers the areas of Parenthood, Development, and Family and Community.

It is written for students studying GCSE Home Economics (Child Development), and will be suitable for a wide variety of related courses including GCSE Home Economics (Home and Family), family and community care courses, and basic sociology courses.

Stanley Thornes

Old Station Drive
Leckhampton
CHELTENHAM
Glos. GL53 0DN

ISBN 0-85950-928-1

9 780859 509282